Ray

M000072607

...thousands of people
from all walks of life
successfully take charge of their careers.

Here's a small sampling of letters Dr. Kevane
has received from clients:

"[Your book] is going to be required reading for my children who are now in high school and college. I want them to benefit from your insight as to how to avoid the process by which people customarily stumble into their careers and job situations.

I saw the career processes of myself, my wife, and my friends described in virtually every page ...

My hope for my children is that they will not fall into the career and job traps that have befallen so many people, including myself, along the way. I believe your book will go a long way toward giving them the insight they need."

> *Steven H. Hughes*
> *Attorney at Law*
> *Hillsboro, Oregon*

"EXCEPTIONALLY SUCCESSFUL! ... FAR BEYOND MY HIGH EXPECTATIONS! ... These spirited words only begin to express my indebted view of your career development program. Without question, it is *very* effective. Thanks to your program, I successfully developed a career strategy which is far exceeding my wishes. I can personally attest to the value of your sound advice and guidance ... Every aspect of your career program is useful, from the first to the last."

> *David Moss, Office Manager*
> *Brown and Caldwell Consultants*
> *Portland, Oregon*

"It really is possible to do *anything* you want ..."
Paul J. Gunis, Entrepreneur
Costa Mesa, California

"...You encouraged me to look at alternatives and, based on my interests and research, make a decision. In effect, you helped me to recognize my options and choose what was right for me ... "
Michael W. Noblet, President
Health Cost Management
Bothell, Washington

" ... Your program is an essential key to my career development. Your program has opened up a new world of possibilities and I find myself thinking that my aspirations are at last achievable.

I am amazed at how easy it is to implement your techniques and methods, and equally amazed at the results they bring forth.

Thank you again for conveying to me the secrets of success and happiness."
Meridyth Burnett,
Seattle, Washington

"I'm happy to report that the ship has landed, and in a magnificent area ... I think this is what you were talking about, doing something from the heart? It sure feels great to be here and working again ...

Thank you for your help and guidance. It sure helped to carry me through some difficult times, and on to something I'd only dreamed of ..."
Rich Robertson, Station Manager
KOWL-AM, KRLT-FM
South Lake Tahoe, California

From Dr. Kevane's colleagues:

"In my years as a professional career consultant, I have found that the career development programs and interview methods developed by Dr. Ray Kevane far surpass any other I have encountered. I have used these methods personally and trained others in their use ..."

Judith G. Louderback, Career Consultant
Louderback & Associates
Seattle, Washington

"It is important that we occasionally acknowledge those who have contributed to our development and success. Your assistance has been invaluable to my company. Thank you.

Your concept of The Self-Directed Career[SM] approach allows our clients to take charge of their lives, increase their productivity, gain in job satisfaction and most importantly, open doors to additional opportunity.

Perhaps the most exciting aspect of your approach is:

IT WORKS!

... Thank you, again, for everything you have done ..."

Fred M. Fredline, Director
F.M. Fredline & Associates
Career Consultants
Chesteron, Indiana

EMPLOYMENT POWER

TAKE CONTROL OF YOUR CAREER

Dr. Raymond A. Kevane

PEANUT BUTTER
PUBLISHING

Seattle, Washington

Copyright © 1994 by Raymond A. Kevane
All rights reserved.

Except for quotations excerpted for critical review, no part of this book may be reproduced or transmitted in any form or by any means, electronic or mechanical, including photocopying, recording, or by any information or referral system, without written permission from the author or the publisher.

The Self-Directed Career℠ is a service mark registered by Raymond A. Kevane. Its use is encouraged with the stipulation that it be identified as "a service mark of Raymond A. Kevane, author and publisher."

The purpose of this book is to educate. Neither the author nor Peanut Butter Publishing nor their affiliates shall have liability or responsibility to any person or entity with respect to damage caused, or alleged to be caused, directly or indirectly, by the use of information contained in this work.

Printed in the United States of America.
33.0014

ISBN 0-89716-501-2

Library of Congress Catalog Card Number:
93-87442

Cover Design: David Marty
Editor: Martha McDonough

Published by:

Peanut Butter Publishing
226 Second Avenue West
Seattle, WA 98119
(206) 281-5965

Dedication

This book is respectfully dedicated to all the clients the author has had the privilege to work with over a period of twenty-two years, and to those who are to come. The courage and tenacity of these remarkable people has been and continues to be a source of deep satisfaction and personal inspiration.

Table of Contents

CHAPTER FOUR

CHAPTER FIVE

CHAPTER SIX

CHAPTER SEVEN

CHAPTER EIGHT

CHAPTER NINE

CHAPTER TEN

CHAPTER ELEVEN

CHAPTER TWELVE

CHAPTER THIRTEEN

OUTPLACEMENT CASE STUDIES

Acknowledgments

My Wife and Family

My wife, Lillian, has given me unwavering support throughout twenty-two years of career consulting work, with its ups and downs, and through the years spent in the writing and production of this book. Without her help and support, neither our career consulting practice nor this book would have come to be.

Very special thanks also go to my children, Karen, Mark and Mary, for the remarkable level of understanding, support and help which they have given.

My Colleagues and Co-Workers

Among the people who have worked with me in our offices in promoting and providing our career guidance services, two stand out for the excellence of their work, their loyalty and their friendship: James Ellis and Donna Klover. My sincerest thanks to each of them.

Advisory Board Members

At both our locations, in Seattle, Washington, and Portland, Oregon, a group of stalwart supporters were members of our advisory boards. These men and women contributed many hours of their time through many years to help us develop and improve our career guidance services. They are Ted Austin; Norm Geersten; Ron Hillbury; Heather Kesten; Kathy Marshack; John Nichols; Lloyd Peterson; Darlene Simpson; Don Weege; Merle Whiteman; and Fred Wist. These are my very good friends. I owe them much.

continued ...

Those Who Helped Produce This Book

It is a remarkable team of people who gathered for the final reworking, editing, publishing, and promotion of this book. My very special thanks to Elliott Wolf, my publisher, whose enthusiasm for the book and its subject matter was a much-needed shot in the arm. Martha McDonough, my editor, has been, I believe, a very unusual editor in the time and attention she gave to the task and in her grasp of the subject matter. David Marty produced this beautiful and striking cover design, which so well epitomizes the pages within. Margaret Liddiard, publicist, has worked tirelessly and effectively in the promotional efforts she has been responsible for. And there are many, many other friends and co-workers who have provided, and continue to provide, support and help.

PREFACE

It is becoming generally recognized that the people who stand out in any field are those who enjoy their work. They find satisfaction in the full range of their career endeavors because of the way in which those activities challenge individual talents, fire the imagination, require creativity, and instill a sense of pride — while also providing more than adequate compensation.

This book is designed to help *you* freely pursue career goals chosen on the basis of talent and desire, even in tough economic times. In the chapters ahead, you'll find guidance in reassessing your relationship to job, business and career, and in developing an attitude of independence in career decision making.

There are a number of forces at work in our country that reduce our freedom when it comes to the way we use our talents and make a living. Those forces — historical, cultural, educational, governmental, and familial — and strategies for overcoming them are discussed in this book.

The cornerstone of the following chapters is The Self-Directed Career℠, a philosophy that places each one of us in charge of our own destinies. It should be remembered that the attitudes which permit personal independence in career must be carefully nurtured and strengthened. The methods which allow for professional movement in the market must be studied, practiced and perfected by each individual. Some readers will find these methods easier to learn and use than others. It must be understood that the growth of professionalism in personal career development, as in any professional capability, will occur over a period of time, involving a good deal of learning and practice.

Just as with any professional undertaking, it is advisable for you to have a coach or a mentor who can help identify mistakes and provide support during the learning process.

CHAPTER ONE

The Present and Future Need: Prepare for Change

*If one advances confidently in the
direction of his dreams....
he will meet with success
unexpected in common hours.*
— Henry David Thoreau

The typical 18 year old in America today will go on to change careers (not just jobs) an average of six or seven times in his or her lifetime. A growing number of sources is making that prediction. I believe it may even be a conservative estimate.

We are in the midst of change. It is accelerating at a dizzying pace. And while change is a constant in life, few of us handle it with comfort. To handle what is coming, we need to regain a vitality which we have lost: The ability to cope with change.

It is easy to forget that major change is a fact of life.

My father and mother were born in 1886, into the horse and carriage era. The telephone and radio were in their infancy. During their lives, my parents saw the automobile come into existence. They read news stories about the first powered airplane flight. They saw the development of the jet plane, then space flight. They watched the first moon-walk on television.

They lived through the first world war and the boom and bust of the '20s and '30s. They suffered the anguish of some of their children enlisting in the second world war. They saw the wars in Korea and Vietnam.

The computer age began in the last years of their lives, but they had no idea what changes it would bring to society.

Their lives more or less paralleled the Industrial Revolution. They not only survived, but flourished in the midst of major change in society. They simply looked to the future with hope, secure in their faith in themselves. They knew they could and would adjust.

Oddly enough, the changes wrought by the Industrial Revolution make it difficult for us today to cope with change. We became the workforce in large corporations, the bureaucrats in government, and the products of the educational system that prepared us for both. In that process, we became dependent on these institutions. Have we become a co-dependent nation? Sadly, I think we have.

Current events are forcing that dependency to end, like it or not. Companies across the country are down-sizing. Some of the giants are under great strain. New industries are coming into being, while old ones are disappearing. Our society is restructuring itself on a global basis.

Eventually, this will benefit us as individuals and as a nation.

The crescendo of layoffs and announcements of layoffs is issuing a wake-up call that none of us dares to ignore. The trend is toward creating smaller companies, and employing fewer people at all levels of business.

The new era — variously called the Information Explosion, the Knowledge Revolution, etc. — is causing an upheaval in the tectonic plates of society. The Industrial Revolution in retrospect looks like a minor rumble.

As these changes occur, we as individuals must learn to compete in the marketplace. To do so requires us to broaden our horizons, and search out a greater span of alternatives.

It was a mistake ever to relinquish responsibility for our own security to an organization, no matter how large its size. This shirking of our responsibility makes poor human (and business) sense. It cripples us mentally and emotionally. It also prevents us from moving into that full maturity that comes only with taking full control of our own destinies.

Years of social programming have created in us attitudes and methods which result in the standard job search. It is an antiquated approach. Our parents implanted it in most of us. The education system reinforced it.

It's business as usual in the halls of education. Teach students in the usual way, knowing that 18 months after graduation, their knowledge will be outdated. Train them in the outdated methods of searching for jobs. Prepare them simply to use the outdated standard job-hunt methods. Instruct them in the use of educational credentials and resumes, which are tools of the past. Equip them to be employees. Prepare them to be subservient to the system.

**To handle what is coming,
we need to regain a vitality which we have lost:
The ability to cope with change.**

A growing number of hardy souls is surfacing. There are those who take matters into their own hands. We see the occasional person who takes control, who makes plans for a career beyond Boeing (or Sears, or IBM, Frederick & Nelson, the auto companies ... and many others).

This is the person who develops his or her own goals. It is the one who learns how to search out and create a professional relationship with an employer, or the one who knows how to found and develop a business.

If courageous people like these can have the attention they deserve, it will inspire others to follow their example.

The wave of the future will be individuals who know professionally how to move in the market. It will be those who develop their ability to find or create their own means of income.

The indomitable spirit which carried my parents and their generation through the changes of the Industrial Revolution is nearly dormant in the American people. It must rise again, and I believe it will rise again.

There are signs now of a grass-roots movement, a groundswell of adjustment to the changes. Like teenagers who feel too restricted by our parents, we are realizing that our dependency on job, company, government, and education is restricting us. We are flexing our muscles, but we don't quite know how to use them yet.

We must revert to the indomitable self-sufficiency which developed this country. It is the same spirit which brought the pioneers from East to West. We need once again to realize that we will find our security simply in ourselves.

We must regain our ability to control our own destinies, our lives and our careers.

It is essential that we develop our personal professionalism. This means that we be able to act with personal initiative; that we accurately project our true strengths and abilities without offending; that we regain our individual self-sufficiency and independence.

We must recover our capacity to make changes when change is upon us.

"... It seems that before each period of change or growth, you go through a lot of pain and doubt. I've learned to accept this and use it in my favor. Every time things get difficult I know that something good will come out of it ..."

D. B., Client

"... Too often before, I settled for any job just for the sake of not being unemployed. That's a lousy reason to get up every morning. Your rigorous approach of having the individual define their job rather than accepting someone else's job needs is both obvious and profound. Too many people stop short, however, of what they want. Thanks for helping me keep my goals first! ..."

D. P., President
___ Equipment Inc.
Seattle, Washington

CHAPTER TWO

Controlling Your Own Career Moves

*When we freely pursue a destiny
we have chosen because it encompasses
our own ideas and ideals,
we will be happiest and most productive.*

◆ Moving Against the Current

Anyone who is truly serious about his or her career must have the courage of personal convictions. Most careers are "other directed" — i.e., they are pursued because we allow ourselves to be pushed into a specific career direction which then becomes a permanent way of life.

Most of us are "programmed" into the type of job we are in, and into the methods required to seek jobs. (See Chapter Four, "Avoiding the Standard Job Hunt.")

If we are to be truly "self-directed" in life, career and job, there is required a complete reversal of the attitude and method instilled in us by society. Instead of a passive role, in which employers (through representatives, such as a personnel department) are permitted to examine and evaluate our background, there is required the eminently *active* role, in which we communicate, not what we have done somewhere else (the resume and standard interview), but rather, our internal talents and abilities as they pertain to a given situation.

This, of course, is difficult. Communication among people is generally hazardous. When it has to do with things which are internal to each of us (such as talents, personal needs, desires, etc.), it becomes more difficult because these are abstractions. It requires special handling to communicate abstractions, such as to teach a course in philosophy. Teaching a course in automotive mechanics, which allows for concrete diagrams and models, is less demanding. When the abstractions pertain to ourselves, it is an even greater challenge. Complicating the problem still further is the fact that we never study, nor are we encouraged to study, how to communicate who we really are.

Teachers are required to study how to communicate in class-rooms. Lawyers and judges must be licensed to communicate in courts of law and generally in the legal profession. Companies require their employees to learn how to communicate the benefits of washing machines to customers, stocks and bonds to a special-ized clientele, insurance policies to potential customers, and so on in an unending list. But we are never encouraged nor taught how to communicate the most complex entity on Earth: Ourselves. Instead, in the job search context, we are encouraged to recite our past activities. We should instead communicate the internal talents and abilities which we carry around within us at all times, and which enabled us to do whatever it is we have done to this point in our lives.

When it comes to job and career, we are taught to be emi-nently *rational* and *practical* in making those decisions. School-ing, years of experience, and other historical considerations (such as family circumstances and social setting), dictate the kind of job we should seek. On the other hand, there are emotion-laden situ-ations, such as the decision to marry, in which it is difficult to be rational and practical.

Any truly valid decision must be based on the whole person — not only the rational side of us, but also the emotional/volitive side. However, we are so conditioned to be entirely *reasonable* in job and career activities that it is relatively impossible without special effort to allow ourselves to identify what we *want* to do. It is from the emotional/volitive part of our natures that our convic-tions come. And when we do something out of conviction and a sense of personal pride, we are at our most enthusiastic, impres-sive and energetic.

Many forces militate against any other approach to career decisions than the rational. The existing system simply calls for a recitation of past experiences upon which managers can base a decision about who should be invited to apply for a job. Or, a series of social adages lock us into place: "It's a lousy job, but I cry all the way to the bank," "A job isn't supposed to be fun," "At least it supports my family," "At least I get two days off a week and a vacation once a year," (Teachers: "It certainly is nice to have the summers off"), "Of course I like what I do — would I have spent 25 years doing it if I didn't?" and so on and on ...

**It's about time we all took charge of our careers ...
not a task that's easily achieved,
but one that is certainly achievable.**

Social forces operate so strongly on all of us that it becomes, as I said, relatively impossible for us to clearly identify what we *want* to do, what we can enjoy, what we can take *pride* in, what we can be *enthusiastic* about.

The following pages are devoted to helping you divest yourself of the restricting forces, both internal and external, which ultimately reduce freedom of career choice.

When we freely decide what we *want* to do and know how to pursue that goal professionally, we are the satisfied, fulfilled practitioners of the Self-Directed Career℠.

◆ The Self-Directed Career℠

Let's face it, when it comes to career, most of us are locked into the problem of ego identification.

The harder we work to be what's expected of us, the more we lose sight of ourselves and our personality. This is especially true of highly competent people who easily master whatever they tackle. Rather than suiting their career to their personality, they strive, often vainly, to tailor their personality to a career. It is an awful way to live.

It's about time we all took charge of our careers. This is a glib statement to be sure, and not a task that's easily achieved, but one that is certainly achievable.

An example: I once worked with a man who had been employed for 18 years by one of America's largest companies. He was very good at what he did and had advanced quickly through the ranks. He had job security and was making good money. He loved his job (he said) but was having problems with his marriage.

The fact was, he hated his work. The resentment he felt towards the job was being transferred to his wife and children. However, since he was a success by work-ethic standards, he developed a denial mindset that said, "The job is great — the problem is my wife."

Once he came to the realization (through intensive reflection) that the opposite was the case, he broke away from the job, placed himself in a position better suited to his talents, and his marital problems cleared up. What's more, even though he was making less money, the personal and life-style adjustments brought on by the change allowed him to save more of his money than he ever had saved before.

This man was saddled with an all-too-common combination of personality traits that forces us to succumb to societal pressure and to be content with our jobs. He also had the typically American attitude that if you do a good job, some wealthy potentate will recognize your talent, elevate you to a higher position, and reward you with more money. Dreams give way to the pressure to make more money than your neighbor or to societal expectations of being a "good provider." A career, rather than being an integration of one's unique talents for the attainment of personal goals, becomes nothing more than a series of jobs.

Sound familiar? I'm sure many of you reading this will think it does. You're probably also wondering what you can do about it.

Start by constantly questioning yourself. **First, are you really using your best talents?** Are you using your latent talents? We tap into only 10 to 20 percent of our potential in a lifetime. Until we tap into the rest of that potential, we're unlikely to be satisfied.

Second, are you being honest about your feelings for what you're doing now, or are you giving in to the pressures outlined earlier? Are you feeling trapped? None of us does our best work when we're feeling trapped. Are you entering the job market for the first time? Are your fears of rejection keeping you from making the contacts you need to make? It is important to face and manage that fear.

Third, question your level of commitment. How willing are you to take the steps necessary to make a change?

If you conclude from all of this questioning that a change in career is the proper destination, there are many different roads you can take to get there. Two things you *don't* want to do, however, are to approach a friend in the wrong way or take a vocational preference test.

Friends, unfortunately, all too often will tell you what they think you want to hear. Or they'll say something like, "With your talent, you should have found something weeks ago." They mean this as a compliment, but it's probably going to make you feel worse.

Standardized vocational preference tests are designed to take your input, which may be less than objective, and compare that input with various common denominators of people in various occupations. These tests become crutches, take away the onus of decision making, and fail to consider many intangibles.

For instance, a survey some years back found that 89 percent of all nurses were unhappy with their jobs. If a preference test found that you were best suited to be a nurse (because you share many common denominators with nurses), it would be steering you toward a job in which you would have a nine in ten chance of being unhappy.

So, what to do?

First, you must learn how to communicate effectively what your abstract talents are. Second, you must develop the ability to teach others about yourself. Third, your product (you) must sell itself. That is, you must know your product and believe in it. Finally, you need an effective means of getting the message across. (More on that in subsequent chapters.)

This process can be learned. There are no guarantees that it will be easy, but as Thoreau said, "If one advances confidently in the direction of his dreams, and endeavors to live the life which he has imagined, he will meet with a success unexpected in common hours."

If it's true that we tap into only 10 to 20 percent of our potential during our lives, then the amount of talent that's wasted in this world is truly incomprehensible.

◆ Identifying Internal Talents

If it's true that we tap into only 10 to 20 percent of our potential during our lives, then the amount of talent that's wasted in this world is truly incomprehensible. Just imagine how much more productive, how much more creative, how much happier the world would be if we could all just identify our internal talents (innate abilities) and channel them into our careers. If only it were that easy.

Make no mistake — we *all* have talents. Unfortunately, most of us never really recognize them. Or worse, we mistake a skill (something learned and developed by repetitive action) for a talent.

For example, someone can develop a skill for working with numbers and become a successful accountant, all the while suppressing a talent for writing. Such a person is likely to feel bored and unfulfilled with accounting, a clear sign that internal talents aren't being tapped.

How, then, to identify your talents? It's pretty much just a matter of opening your mind to possibilities. Dream a little bit. Envision yourself doing something else. How does it feel? Do you see yourself being happy and comfortable? If so, chances are you have (or can develop) a talent for whatever it is you're envisioning.

Of course, you have to be realistic. Many of us might find it easy to envision ourselves as a movie star or professional athlete, but few of us genuinely have the talent to be one. At the same time, the accountant I alluded to might comfortably envision him or herself as a copywriter or reporter.

Next, examine what you do with your life outside your job. Your hobbies and interests will provide some concrete clues as to where your talents lie, since few of us spend our leisure time doing things we don't enjoy or aren't good at. Of course, don't forget that people sometimes ruin good hobbies by trying to make money at them.

However, the man who works with tools and machines all day, then spends his weekends fixing up old cars, probably has a talent for working with equipment and machinery.

On the other hand, I once worked with a man who had spent years in facilities management. (Basically, he supervised janitorial services.) In his private life, he was the president of a national volunteer organization. This man had immense talents for leadership and management that he was not using in his income-producing life.

Next, take a hard, *honest* look at your self-image. It's purely subjective, of course, but to a large extent, it's probably reasonably accurate. If your self-image is too low or too high, it's likely because you're not using your talents. (Or meeting your internal requirements — more on that just ahead.)

Take a hard look at your conditioned reflexes — the habit patterns which you have formed after years of repetitive action. They could be a clue to your talents. Are you better at formulating policy or carrying out plans? Do you work better with things or with people? With numbers or with words? Alone or as part of a team? (Bear in mind, if you undertake this exercise, the work you do and have done will influence your functional patterns. If you've been in military service for 30 years, your *modus operandi* will be substantially different from someone who's spent 30 years in retail sales. But, properly attended to, these habits can be modified.)

Even take a look at the things you enjoyed as a child, before you faced the pressure of parents and teachers trying to mold you into someone you're not. People often suppress their personal desires (talents?) for the purpose of trying to please their parents. This is especially true for the children of professionals, who commonly feel that they must be professionals as well.

In the course of all this self-examination, you may very well find that you are using your basic talents in your career. The broader question then becomes: Are you using them in the best application? If not, perhaps it's time to look for something better.

Particularly applicable in this context is a fable about a youth sitting in a fig tree, surrounded by ripe, juicy figs, yet who starves to death because he can't decide which one to eat. Many talented people are like that youth, sitting in a fig tree (their job) and slowly starving for fear of losing money, security or ego, while their figs (better opportunities) rot within arm's reach. Don't let yourself be one of those people. Learn more about the full range of your internal talents and set out immediately to start using them. You will certainly be much happier for it.

◆ Identifying Internal Requirements

Unlike a washing machine or a loaf of bread, each of us cares who "buys" our abilities. But we try hard not to care.

"I can't stand my job," says the comedian, "but I'm laughing all the way to the bank."

It's a sad commentary on modern life that this line never fails to get a laugh. Many people don't like the work they do, but they do it for money or social pressure, in the belief that it's okay to hate their work because, after all, a job isn't supposed to be fun.

What nonsense! If you're not happy with your job, chances are it doesn't meet your internal requirements, the combination of needs and personality traits that make you unique. It's high time that you identified the things that are important to you and set about placing yourself in a position where they're being satisfied.

If you're a square peg trying to squeeze yourself into a round hole, you're going to be miserable. If you're trying to mold yourself into a round peg, you'll be no better off.

Unfortunately, I can't give you ten easy steps for identifying your needs. It's a matter of doing a great deal of introspection and bouncing things off of people who are close to you or are trained in such matters. It could well be the most difficult task you'll ever undertake, since, for a variety of reasons, we often suppress our needs rather than face them squarely.

(I'm reminded of a client who repeatedly denied that he needed money and who, despite the fact that he was extremely talented, consistently placed himself in jobs that barely paid him enough to feed his family. It turns out that this man's father was a strict disciplinarian who believed it was wrong for anyone to earn more than what one needed for survival. Having forgotten that his father ever said such a thing, this man was still unconsciously obeying his father. Realizing this was a shocking and life-altering revelation for him.)

Here, then, is a sampling of internal requirements, or personal needs — that we all have to one degree or another. Use them as thought-starters toward identifying your own.

1. Leadership. Aggressive personalities in particular have a need for leadership and will fight for it. At the same time, there are many who deny or suppress this need.

2. Independence. Some people were meant to be running their own businesses, or at least, they require broad latitude as employees.

3. Advancement. This word is commonly misapplied. Most people think it means a raise or a promotion. In fact, it means some form of personal growth. Most of us have never identified the ways in which we want to grow.

4. Surroundings. Think of the forest rangers you've met. Can you picture them being happy in an office job? Safety is a real concern for some people. Healthful surroundings can also be important. It may be important for you to have high respect for those you work with and for you to be equally respected in return.

5. Social interaction with co-workers. Is this important to you? Many people prefer not to socialize off-hours with co-workers.

6. Security. Whether in terms of money, ego, or protection from job loss, this need often overrides all others. Obviously, a debt-ridden man with children in the hospital will have a justifiably strong need for security. Most of the rest of us place too much importance on it.

7. Ethics (professionalism). Some people are deeply concerned about the values and practices of the business they work for. This has been demonstrated lately in the growing number of people who, at great personal risk, report injustices and illegal practices performed by their organization.

8. Status. Most people deny they have a need for status because of the negative connotation society places on the word. Properly defined, status is important to all of us. Think of it as your standing with reference to something outside yourself, with that something selected strictly by you.

9. Geography (roots). Some people have a need to stay put. Others need to keep moving and exploring new areas.

10. Creativity. This is one of the most difficult of needs to define, as one person's creativity is another person's boredom. What's more, companies tend to stifle creativity by drawing up job descriptions and molding people into them. Highly creative people often substitute doing a number of different things for creativity and become chronic job-hoppers. They move around for the excitement of doing something new rather than because the new job is right for them.

11. Income. It may be true that money can't buy happiness, but for whatever reason, some of us need more of it than others. Contrary to appearances, most people put high income rather low on the list — after they really think it through.

Once you have identified your needs, open your mind to job possibilities that would meet those needs. Dream a little.

The person who tries to pattern his or her career according to personal requirements, all things else being equal, will do a better job for the employer. But remember that *you* are the only person who can determine what your needs are. And remember that you *must* determine what you need before you can look for it.

♦ Identifying Your Personal Desires

In Chapter Six are some thoughts on developing your ability to communicate your true self as a key to a successful career. Communicating your true self, of course, is easier said than done, particularly in an interview setting or in an employee/boss relationship. I believe these are among the most difficult settings in which we try to communicate, given the pressure each situation brings to bear on the individual.

Most bosses, after all, are good at giving orders, running meetings and refereeing disputes. Rarely are they trained in interpersonal skills, and even more rarely do they know how to conduct an interview. Therefore, during an interview, they fall back on using a resume (job history) as a means of examining the person on the other side of the desk. This puts the interviewee in a passive role — sitting back and waiting to be questioned.

But communication in its truest sense is a positive, *active* process. This is true whether it involves communicating a subject matter in a classroom (teaching), communicating washing machines to householders (selling), or projecting oneself across a desk to be more fully understood by an employer (self-communication). None of us can communicate effectively unless we exercise a minimum level of control over *what* is communicated and *how* it is communicated.

An interviewee is trying to "sell" the most complex and sophisticated product on Earth: A human being. In addition, an interview is a marketing situation in which the seller (the interviewee) cares very deeply about who "buys" the product (although too many people pretend that they don't care). And it's the only marketing situation I know of in which the product literally must sell itself. You can't send in a proxy to do the interview for you or send a product sample for the interviewer to try on his or her own time.

So you find yourself in a pressure-filled situation, trying to sell something incredibly complex and totally abstract — your talents — and to buy something which will satisfy something that is equally as complex and abstract — your needs. The chances are, no matter how good a salesperson (and buyer!) you are, you can't do it. It's exceedingly rare to find the person who has really studied himself or herself with the kind of depth and honesty needed to communicate one's true self. (Beyond that, it is equally rare to find the person who has studied and developed the professional skill required to project that true self effectively. Both are necessary; both can be learned and developed.)

How do you gain this kind of self-knowledge? The fastest and surest way is to enlist the services of someone who knows how to help. And there are many self-help books around that can help you open some of your inner doors. But in substance, it's a matter of a great deal of introspection. As you go through this process, it's also important to honestly acknowledge where your true interests lie. Too often, people deny their true interests and fall back on their training or cave in to family pressure. But if you have a clear vision of what you want and a determination to get there, it will make it all that much easier to communicate your true self to others.

Having gone through this process, you then need to do the following:

1. Acknowledge in what field your true interests lie.

2. Carefully examine that field to determine what price you will have to pay in order to enter it and succeed in it.

3. Determine whether you're willing to pay that price.

4. Don't give up.

It may not be practical for you to be a starving artist if you have children to feed and a mortgage to pay. On the other hand, you may be able to go back to school or work a second job while you pursue whatever plans you've devised.

**The interview is the only marketing situation
in which the product literally must sell itself.
You can't send in a proxy to do the interview for you
or send a product sample for the interviewer to try
on his or her own time.**

Too often it is merely the fear of the unknown that keeps people from pursuing their dreams. However, nothing is more impressive than the individual who is absolutely determined to make something work and won't be stopped until it does. And that is most definitely a part of communicating yourself.

There's an old saying, "If you think you can or you think you can't, either way you're right." It's the absolute truth when it comes to communicating your true self and being at your most credible with an employer.

" ... Your program helped me to identify personal internal needs and wants and provided a mechanism of demonstrating these abstract talents in terms of career capabilities ... "

C. H., Client

"... The personal issues we covered have helped me gain a better insight into the real me. This includes a better understanding of my tendencies, and how I can put them to the most effective use. I frequently feel a sense of accomplishment in my work."

D. M., Client

CHAPTER THREE

Examining the "Shape of the Peg"

Know Thyself.
— Socrates

The Truth Will Set You Free.
— Jn. 8,32

♦ Reversing the System of Finding Jobs

Current jargon suggests that there are many "square pegs in round holes" in our society — or *vice versa*. This refers, of course, to the number of people in the U.S. marketplace who are not comfortable in their jobs. Statistics tell us, in various ways, that 80 to 90 percent of workers feel this way, with emotions ranging from relatively strong discomfort to intense, persistent stress. The causes of this discomfort/stress are innumerable, varying in some degree from person to person.

This problem is perpetuated because the job-hunting system requires a person to describe all the jobs ("holes") he or she has occupied and find another of at least similar shape. So a person leaves one uncomfortable setting and finds another.

The only way this can be alleviated (beyond the sheerest kind of luck) is to reverse the system we have long been taught to use and begin — not by looking for a job similar to those we have had — but by studying the "shape of the peg." In other words, each of us should first examine our own hopes and aspirations, and our talents and abilities as they reside within us; clarify our personal and career values; and, armed with this knowledge, determine where in the entire marketplace we are likely to find the position ("hole") which will fit us (the "peg"). Or, rather than relying on extrinsic evidence (degrees, training, experience), we should depend upon intrinsic evidence to make the decision.

The definition of our career is not out in the marketplace where jobs are listed. It is not in our backgrounds. The definition of a valid career for each of us lies *within* each of us. Honest self-knowledge is difficult to achieve. But very few things equal it in importance.

♦ The Strongest People Recognize Their Weaknesses.

Two kinds of self-deception prevent us from achieving all that we can. The first kind of self-deception is false modesty, and it is usually practiced by people who have many talents but are afraid to reveal them because they would be expected to use those talents. A second kind of self-deception is denial. While people who deny that they have weaknesses appear at first to be extremely confident and capable, they are often the first to crack under stress. Because they fail to admit their weaknesses, they never correct them or learn to compensate for them.

The most successful people are those who are able to accurately assess their strengths and weaknesses, then capitalize on their strengths and compensate for their weaknesses.

I once worked with a top executive of a major company who made daily decisions involving monumental amounts of money and numerous people. He was one of the strongest, most confident people I have known. The key to his strength was his willingness to listen intently to anybody because he felt he still had much to learn. He understood his strengths and weaknesses, and he was content with himself.

Accurately assessing strengths and weaknesses is difficult. Friends and family members usually know a lot about our strengths and weaknesses, but they are reluctant to share their knowledge for fear of offending us. In addition, because individual perceptions and situations vary, the feedback received from one source, such as a friend, may contradict the feedback received from another source, such as a boss. As a result, understanding our own strengths and weaknesses requires that we regularly "step outside ourselves" and examine our strengths and weaknesses as objectively as possible. Here are a few ways to do that:

Look at what interests you. Generally, whenever people have a dedicated interest in a field, they can be truly outstanding in that endeavor if they are willing to develop their talents. A good example of this is the man who for many years had been an engineer at a manufacturing firm and gradually grew more dissatisfied. He was tired of engineering; he wanted to interact more with other people. Eventually, he left the company and accepted a communications position where his day-to-day contact with people was greatly increased. Because the job required very different skills from his previous position, he experienced a good deal of anxiety. However, he dedicated himself to redeveloping his people skills, and as he became more comfortable in his new role, he found that he was enjoying work more than he had in years.

Listen to what other people say about you. This seems very simple, but there is an amazing number of people who embark on their most fulfilling career path after being told for many years that they had a talent in that area. Many of us tend to brush off compliments from family members and friends, thinking that they are prejudiced and that their perceptions are therefore invalid. But these are usually the people who know us best. They often are aware of talents or interests that casual acquaintances, co-workers or bosses would never see.

Take time out occasionally to reevaluate your strengths and weaknesses. As we grow and mature, our strengths and weaknesses change. What may have been challenging a few years ago may be routine today. Recognize that some changes may be temporary. Even the most socially bold extrovert has to walk on the beach alone once in a while, and the most introverted person occasionally needs human company. Other changes may be more permanent.

Select a confidant carefully. Some people feel threatened when friends make drastic changes, particularly if they are themselves unhappy. Most people don't intend their negative comments to be harmful, but jealousy can lead to acrimony.

**Any reasonably talented person
who is willing to make the commitment
to true self-honesty
is capable of rising far beyond
his or her current situation.**

Socrates said, "Know thyself." He might have gone on to say that knowing thyself is a lifetime quest. The only way to begin is to acknowledge that there are many ways in which we don't know ourselves, and then make a conscious effort to change that.

Any reasonably talented person who is willing to make this commitment — who has the self-honesty and determination to capitalize on strengths and overcome weaknesses — is capable of rising far beyond his or her current situation.

◆ Career Value Systems

A fundamental concern is that too many people base their career choices on an intellectual assessment of their experience (and how much money they'll make), rather than on their own internal needs and internal talents. Needs and talents should be the two most important factors in career decisions.

Always implicit and even more basic, however, is a third factor: Values.

Every one of us has a value system, but few of us ever independently adopt our own or articulate what we adopt. Most people simply adopt a typically American value system that was born of the pioneer spirit and magnified in the Depression. This value system places the pursuit of security (wealth?) above everything.

It's passed along from parent to child, from teacher to student, and from boss to employee.

Values, as I use the word here, are an overriding set of guiding principles that help us determine what is appropriate behavior. From these personal values, we can derive our career values. As with needs and talents, if our career values don't mesh with our job, we're likely to be unhappy.

Whether we are conscious of them or not, of course, we have always had a set of personal values. In general, we aren't conscious of those values unless confronted with situations that challenge them.

Values are an overriding set of guiding principles that help us determine what is appropriate behavior. From these, we can establish our career values.

And while most Americans find it easy to stand up for their values in personal life, most will swallow their personal values when they're in conflict with the unethical stance of an employer because of the "security-above-all-else" ethic which is so pervasive in our society.

It doesn't have to be that way. For people who are truly in charge of their careers, it isn't.

To achieve that kind of self-sufficiency, we must first be conscious of what our values are. That doesn't mean we have to question them, only that we be conscious of them.

Then we must ask whether they're really ours, or whether they're someone else's. Our conscious values are likely to be at least partially those of our parents and teachers.

Here's a simple exercise you can try:

Make a list of some of the things you've done that really made you proud, both in the doing and in the accomplishment. The list can be as long as you like. Examine each item and cross out those that made you proud primarily because they pleased your parents, your teachers or your bosses, rather than because they pleased you.

Next, cross out the remaining items that gave you a sense of accomplishment rather than a sense of pride. There's a key difference here and I'm not sure that I can adequately describe it, but let me try:

You may recall a news story a few years ago about the college student who, from publicly available documents, designed and assembled an atomic bomb. That was quite an achievement and if it were me, I would feel an intense sense of accomplishment. I don't know that I'd be very proud of what I had produced, though.

What remains on your list will be those items that genuinely made you proud. Examine each one carefully for the underlying values that gave you that sense of pride, and list them separately. Those values might include, for example, being a benefit to society, lending support to individuals, doing high-quality work, maintaining your ethical posture in spite of pressure ... and so on. When the list is complete, you'll then have some components of your fundamental value system.

You'll also probably find that you place a relatively low value on monetary wealth. More often than not, people simply use money as a means of justifying doing things that conflict with their real values. If you are doing what you can take pride in and have reasonable income for the present which provides reasonably for the future, then money takes on decreasing importance.

Of course, it's up to you to apply your values to your career by examining how a company treats its people, the sales tactics it uses, the work environment it creates, the products it makes, and a host of other issues. This might well create an entirely new vision of what you want out of your job and career.

If you're a business owner or manager, you can think in terms of creating a set of corporate values, a step that most companies never bother to take. After all, values are a human quality and corporations are by definition nonhuman. But identifying values can help a company formulate its goals and develop a better sense of what is expected from everyone who deals with or works for that company.

Your values can be a blend of societal, religious and parental values, but above all, they must be yours. Just as you cannot have a meaningful life without a value system, neither can you have a meaningful career without one.

◆ Success: What is it?

Are you a success? Have you had or are you having a successful career? A lot of people might look at their nice office, their big house, their luxury car and their fat paycheck and answer "yes" ... for the wrong reasons.

Success is the culmination of personal growth. It is the attainment of legitimate internal desires, hopes and aspirations, and the fulfillment of values.

After all, what is success? Many of us are programmed to believe that success is defined simply by the amount of money we make compared to our peers, by the size and value of a house or car, or by our stratum in society. Indeed, it's natural to want to keep up with the Joneses and there's certainly nothing wrong with living comfortably. But too many people get caught up in a rat-race job they can't stand in order to fulfill someone else's vision of success.

I prefer to define success as personal growth, or the continuation of personal growth. It is the attainment of legitimate internal desires, hopes and aspirations, and the fulfillment of values. Money may be a means to this end, but rarely is it an end in itself.

There are and have been people to whom money seemed to be the sole end, but money can also be a ball and chain that enslaves people. As just one example, look at the plethora of desperately unhappy celebrities who wind up in alcohol treatment centers or who take their own lives. Successes? I think not.

In general, successful people are those who are fully in charge of their careers, regardless of how much money they make. They are exceedingly sensitive to career values and are usually independent thinkers who are very objective about themselves. And since they love their work, they tend to be very good at it. So the money follows. Even if it doesn't, I find that successful people don't care. They have, pardon the cliché, what money can't buy: Happiness, contentment, and personal pride.

Back in the early 1970s, I worked with a top-echelon oil company executive who was, by the classic American definition, a success. He made over $200,000 a year (today's equivalent) and lived with his beautiful wife in a big house. But he was ashamed of his company, his marriage was crumbling, and he was desperately unhappy. When he first came to me, it was with the assumption that he needed to place himself in a similar position with another major company. He couldn't have been more wrong.

After some serious soul-searching, he realized that he would never be happy doing what he was doing. He further realized that he had many internal talents and needs that his oil company job did not, and never would, fulfill. When I last heard from him, he was a fully tenured college professor, and he and his wife were happier than they'd ever been. It's the most complete success story I know of.

So I ask again, are you a success? Ask yourself a few questions:

How do you feel when you go to work in the morning and come home at night? Do you wish you didn't have to go to work when you get up? Do you go through a "personality change" at home in the evening? This is common in people who are unhappy with their work.

How do you feel about telling other people what you do? Successful people are proud of what they do.

Is your physical health as good as it's always been? I don't want to render medical opinions, but people who are dealing with bad stress on the job are more susceptible to physical ailments. (Note that there is such a thing as good stress. It's what makes a job challenging and pushes us on to better things.) Again, I don't mean to pass judgment, but is the CEO who's making $500,000 a year and suffering from ulcers and heart problems a success?

How do you feel about your co-workers? Is there an easy camaraderie? Is there mutual respect? Successful people give that respect easily and get it without demanding it.

How do you feel about telling others what you do for a living? Successful people are proud of what they do.

Do molehills appear to be mountains? This is common among people who don't like what they're doing. For successful people, mountains appear to be molehills.

Success is elusive. It rarely comes without hard work and dedication to one's dreams. And the best advice I can give you is that which has been handed down through the centuries: *Be true to yourself.* The truth may hurt, but the truth will set you free.

CHAPTER FOUR

Know What NOT To Do

> *The most effective job searches involve*
> *direct contact with decision makers.*
> *No one can "sell" you to a decision maker*
> *as expertly as you yourself can learn to do.*
> *And no one will represent you*
> *as energetically as you will.*

♦ Avoiding the Standard Job Hunt

It happens to virtually everyone sooner or later: You find yourself out of work, or frustrated with the job you have and ready to find something more fulfilling. Or maybe you've just graduated from high school or college and are looking for your first job. What do you do?

If you're like most people, you start reading the want ads, registering with employment agencies and sending your resume to any and every company that's similar to the one for which you've been working, or that might take a beginner. If you're like most people, you suffer through a long, agonizing wait for a new job.

The standard job hunt, as described above, is a brutally inefficient way to get work. Don't get me wrong, a lot of people find jobs that way, but they tend to be lower level or "holding pattern" jobs. If you're serious about making a career change, or getting started on a meaningful career path, the standard job hunt should be avoided by whatever means possible.

Here's why:

1. The Want Ads. It's generally acknowledged that 80 to 90 percent of *all* positions are filled without ever being advertised. This is true for entry-level positions as well. Hiring someone is an extremely stressful process that can make an employer look like a genius or a fool. So as a rule, employers would rather hire privately, choosing from a pool of people they or their friends know. (After all, the devil you know is better than the devil you don't know.) It's usually only after these private avenues have been exhausted that an ad goes in the paper.

If you do respond to a want ad, it's likely that your resume is one of hundreds that were received. (I was told recently that one Fortune 500 company receives more than 150,000 resumes per year.) Your odds of winning something in the lottery are better than they are of getting an advertised job which really fits you.

Want ads are also not always placed to fill a position. A company might be doing research (i.e., how much to pay a new position), fulfilling legal requirements, or recruiting talent for future openings.

2. Employment agencies. The overwhelming majority of agencies are hard-working, reputable firms that will help you match your experience with whatever openings they have on file. The problem is, they look at your experience, not your talents. If you're looking for a lateral move into a position similar to the one you just left, by all means, register with the employment agencies. But it just won't work if you're looking for a change.

3. Blanket mailings of resumes. Again, if you're looking for a lateral move into a similar position, this might work. But fewer than one percent of all unsolicited resumes result in a job.

4. Networking. A few years ago, this new dimension was (consciously) added to job-search programs. While networking activities increase a person's number of contacts and may help speed up the job search process, they rarely lead to the right kind of position nor do they tap into the broadest range of available positions.

What, then, is a better way to go about doing it? It is important to establish a series of *professional relationships* within a targeted area of the marketplace.

Think back to the typical hiring process described earlier. The employer thinks of all the people he or she knows and talks to friends about all the people they know. The key is to inject yourself into that process; to become one of the people the employer or the employer's friend thinks of.

Determine exactly what it is you want to do, then do a little research to pinpoint where and for whom you'd like to do it. Find out who the people are that make the hiring decisions and develop an orderly, *professional* method of contact. Present your *talents* to them, not your background, and present yourself as a potential profit center. To be effective, you'll need to do three things:

1. Communicate what your talents are. You must be able to present yourself in a direct and readily understandable manner.

2. Teach a potential employer about your product (your talents). To do this, you must know and believe in yourself thoroughly. You must also be presenting yourself to someone who finds your product valuable. (For a teacher to be effective, the students must be interested in the subject.)

3. Market your product. Remember that you're selling something. Take an active, not a passive role. Determine a potential employer's needs and clearly demonstrate how you are uniquely qualified to fill them.

I would guess that 80 to 90 percent of all the decision makers *are* accessible if you can get around their defense mechanisms, the most obvious one being the personnel department.

While they serve many valuable functions, personnel departments, often called "human resources," ironically don't always deal with people. In the hiring process, they mostly deal with pieces of paper. They are not designed to identify people's talents; they're designed to develop job descriptions and find the person whose *experience* most closely fits the description. They also act as a screening service to keep people away from the employer so he or she is free to concentrate on more important tasks.

Once you've gotten through to the decision maker, you will need professional interview methods. (More on that in Chapter Six.) As a necessary prerequisite, however, concentrate on defining precisely what it is you want to do. The more clearly you can draw your target, the easier it will be to hit the bull's-eye.

♦ The Best Resume Is No Resume.

There is NO SUCH THING as an effective resume.

I realize that that statement is heresy in a business world that places a "well-written resume" on a par with a fat profit margin, but it's my opinion that, if you're looking for happiness and a change of direction, the best resume is no resume.

Suppose you saw the following ad for a washing machine:

WASHING MACHINE FOR SALE:

Steel smelted and rolled: Pittsburgh, PA, August, 1985
Motor manufactured: Detroit, MI, December, 1985
Belts and hoses molded: Akron, OH, January, 1986
Machine assembled: Chicago, IL, April, 1986
Shipped to dealer: Houston, TX, February, 1987

Would this ad make you want to run right out and buy this washing machine? Of course not. A salesman who tried to sell washing machines with that ad would starve. But this is exactly how most people structure their resumes. They simply provide a history of themselves that fails to sell their talents and abilities and restricts their vision of the future.

I usually advise people to conduct their job hunts without a resume. It's done by identifying who can benefit from your talents and abilities, approaching the employment decision makers directly, and ensuring that they perceive the benefits you offer.

If, however, you really do need to have something in writing, an alternative to the standard resume is a document that looks like a resume but doesn't name companies or list dates. I call it a "qualifications summary." It identifies your responsibilities and the results you achieved both on and off the job. (Remember, experience is experience whether you've made money at it or not.)

If your resume lists you as "VP/marketing, Brand X Corp., 1978-1987," you're putting yourself in a passive role and hoping that the information will be interpreted correctly by the reader. However, if you use a qualifications summary that states "As VP/marketing for a national distribution firm, I planned and implemented a program that resulted in a 500% increase in sales in a two-year period," a potential employer is likely to think, "Wow! I wonder if he could do that for me?"

One of my favorite examples of a man who used this technique successfully is an Army colonel I worked with many years ago. As a high-ranking officer at a major military installation, he was responsible for all of the housing on the base, and organizing moves and transportation for personnel all over the world. In effect, he ran a very large city.

If his resume had identified him as a 30-year military man, he would have gotten absolutely nowhere. Instead, he developed a qualifications summary in which he identified himself as, "Executive Director of a major unit of a national service organization." He then listed his responsibilities and, more importantly, the results he achieved on the job and the benefits he could offer an employer.

Eventually, he found himself in the running for a position as director of a community action team in a small Northwest city. Throughout the interview process, he flatly (but politely) refused to provide anyone with a work history. It was not until the final interview with the board of directors that he finally revealed that his experience had come in the Army. By that time, though, it was irrelevant. He got the job.

Unfortunately, there are times when you just can't get away from using a resume. A large bureaucracy, for example, probably won't deal with anything that doesn't look like a standard resume.

Similarly, a personnel manager won't know what to make of anything that doesn't list where you worked, when you worked there and what your title was. (That's why it's important to bypass personnel departments and go directly to the decision maker.) If you're making a lateral move, of course, while there is a better way, it will not work entirely against you to use a work history.

If you find yourself caught up in the hiring process, and people start demanding a resume, as happened with the colonel, you have to decide whether to go for broke. If you give in, you lose. People use resumes to find reasons *NOT* to hire someone. I recommend that you hold your ground in a comfortable, courteous way. You're more likely to win.

Resumes provide companies with all the reasons NOT to hire someone.

A few tips about the qualification summary:

First, be careful what you say about your education. Employers will use too much or too little education as an excuse to screen you out.

Second, avoid any mention of dates. It may be against the law to discriminate on the basis of age, but the fact is that it happens. Dates will help employers pinpoint your age.

Lastly, lead off with a *specific* career objective. Don't say you want, "to find a challenging position with a growing company." That says nothing. List the specific responsibilities you want, the specific skills you want to use, and the specific field you want to be in. Then go for it.

♦ **Responding to Newspaper Ads**

Suppose you were a washing machine salesman in a highly competitive market. Suppose further that your only sales effort was a daily examination of the classified ads in your local newspaper, placed by people who want to buy a washing machine. How many do you think you'd sell?

Not many (if any) of course, since householders rarely advertise their intention to buy such items. The rare exception, to my knowledge, is the person who hopes to find a good deal on a used machine from another householder.

This is directly analogous to what happens when job seekers rely on want ads in their local newspaper. Employers don't generally advertise their good positions. The ones they do advertise are likely to be less appropriate to you, and you'll have lots of competition. Granted, there are a lucky handful who find good jobs through want ads, but your odds of getting such a job are poor. And the odds of getting something really suited to you are worse than they are of winning top prize in the lottery.

It cannot be said too often that 80 to 90 percent of all jobs are never advertised. They're filled via private avenues. Those people who put their hopes in want ads invariably wind up in a downward spiral of frustration and depression.

Besides, want ads aren't always placed for the purpose of filling a position. Often, companies are merely complying with equal opportunity laws or board regulations even though a decision on whom to hire was made long before. (I have found this to be especially true of government agencies.) Or they're doing research to find out how much to pay a newly created position. Or employment agencies use ads as a means of bringing new people into their offices.

(Bear in mind that this is true of local newspapers only. Trade publications and business publications such as *The Wall Street Journal* are likely to contain ads from employers with high-quality positions to fill. But they, too, are likely to be inundated with responses.)

The most effective job searches involve direct contact with decision makers. In fact, I usually urge my clients to ignore the want ads.

Being a realist, however, I know that people nonetheless read and respond to ads. As such, here are some tips for doing it more effectively:

1. Have someone else read the ads for you and tell you about those positions that might be of interest to you. That way you can avoid the depression that comes from looking in the paper every day and not seeing anything suited to you.

2. Write each cover letter to suit the specific situation. A standard letter that you send in response to each ad won't get much attention. A letter that addresses, point by point, each of the requirements listed in the ad is more likely to be noticed.

3. Keep your letter brief and to the point. Too many people tend to be verbose and ponderous in their opening paragraphs. "In response to your recent advertisement, I am herewith enclosing a copy of my resume" doesn't quite have the punch of, "I'm a perfect candidate for the job. Here's why."

4. State that you've had the required experience. Employers appear to be looking for the 25 year old with 35 years' experience who'll work for $750 a month. But they're also looking for the person who'll do the best job of solving their problems.

Try something like, "My experience goes far beyond the five years you require." Then be prepared to back it up with facts, even if it is not direct or on-the-job experience.

5. Don't send a resume. I know this is a tough one to swallow since employers and personnel managers can get awfully cranky if they don't have a work history to look at, no matter how irrelevant it may be to defining a person's skills and talents. It could even kill your chances of getting the job.

A better approach, however, is to send a "qualifications summary." (See the previous section on this subject.) This is a document that looks like a resume but does not list titles, dates and companies. Instead it lists a specific career objective, your most significant accomplishments, and reasons why you feel qualified for the position. Each qualification summary must be tailored to the ad you're answering.

6. Don't discuss salary, even if the ad specifically asks for salary requirements. Say you're entirely negotiable on salary, and face the possibility that your application will be rejected because of this.

7. Don't provide references. Instead, end your qualifications summary with a paragraph that says, "References will state that John Doe is hard-working, intelligent, etc., etc." If pressed, provide only the names of people who will say exactly that.

8. Don't get your hopes up.

◆ Employment Agencies and Recruiters

Let me say immediately that the majority of employment agencies and executive search firms are reputable, hard-working organizations who do an excellent job of what they do. In some states they have established a self-policing association to ensure a high level of professionalism.

The problem with agencies and search firms, however (with apologies to my friends in the business), is that they are virtually useless when it comes to helping people who are seeking to take charge of their careers, either by making a major advancement in their current field or by moving to another field entirely. Such firms are best used by people seeking to make lateral moves, but who don't have time to actively job hunt. They can also be helpful to young people looking for their first job.

If you're going to involve agencies and search firms in your career moves, it's best to have a realistic pictu.e of how they work and how to use them to your advantage.

Throughout this, you must remember that their loyalty is to the corporation (the employer), not to the job seeker. No fees are paid until the corporation hires.

And nowadays, it's frequently the corporation that pays for

the service. For agencies and search firms to keep their corporate customers satisfied, they must provide the people with the "right" backgrounds. So let's talk first about employment agencies: Employment agencies will typically scour the market for job openings or learn of openings from regular corporate clients, then advertise those positions. (It is illegal for them to advertise a position that does not exist.)

From the responses they receive, along with the unsolicited resumes that deluge their offices, they will try to find those people whose background and experience most closely match the job description. After signing a contract, these people are sent to employers for interviews. If hired, the individual is obligated to pay the agency fee if the employer does not.

As you can well imagine, if you are not willing to provide a complete, detailed work history, an employment agency is a waste of your time. Some agencies may urge you to work exclusively with them. I would suggest you not do so, but rather register with several. The more professional firms will recommend this. On the other hand, be selective about those agencies you wish to represent you. Talk to the people there, find out how they work, and get a feel for the rapport you can establish with them.

Then be courteously persistent. Call or visit every day — or twice a day. The people who exude confidence, who keep at it, are the people who'll be looked upon more favorably. After all, they'll be easier for the agency to "sell" to a potential employer.

Executive recruiters and search firms operate quite differently than employment agencies. They will not, as a rule, deal with people who come to them looking for work. Like employment agencies, however, they are not paid unless the company hires someone they have referred.

Most recruiters work by establishing personal contacts with the companies they represent and working with those companies to find people who fit their needs. Again, they're more likely to be interested in matching experience and background to job descriptions than in helping someone make a career change.

They will also try to find the right people by advertising as well as networking. A common approach in networking is for a recruiter to call someone who currently holds a position similar to the one he's trying to fill and ask if that person knows of anyone who might be interested. (Of course, he's really asking if that person is interested.)

Eventually, the recruiter will wind up with a list of highly qualified prospects for the employer, who has been spared the trouble of advertising the position and being deluged with resumes.

**Agencies and recruiters
will never sell you to decision makers
as effectively as you will sell yourself —
if you know how.
And they are not geared to help you
make a radical career change.**

It's difficult — perhaps impossible — to use recruiters to your advantage. However, recruiters have loads of contacts in all sorts of businesses, and I suggest you could potentially use a recruiter as a center of influence. You might request a meeting to introduce yourself and provide a broader understanding of your abilities and career goals. Frankly, though, I'd be surprised if many of them agreed to it. Their paycheck comes from the company, not the job seeker, and they know it.

The bottom line, of course, is that agencies and recruiters will never sell you to decision makers as hard as you'd sell yourself. Nor will they help you make a radical career change. For that sort of move, there's only one person who can help you. To find him or her, just look in the mirror.

"... Your guidance through the difficult process of 'deciding what to be when I grew up' and selecting a career path made it possible for me to see it through. It also enabled me to review and analyze the widest possible range of career choices before arriving at the few in which I have the greatest interest ... "

J. M., Seattle

CHAPTER FIVE

Establishing Career (and Life) Directions

*We use our energies best
when they are focused
on a well-chosen objective.*

◆ Career Goal Setting

Goal setting is perhaps the most difficult and intimidating aspect of taking charge of your career. But it's the core issue in all successful careers; everything else revolves around it.

Unfortunately, via education and background, people identify themselves by function, and our society and educational system reinforce the ridiculous notion that we're supposed to choose a function at age 18, train ourselves to be proficient in that function, then work at that function our entire lives. What's more, we're expected to stick with things we're good at, even if we can't stand them.

Words can't begin to describe how preposterous I think this is. To get an idea of how hollow our system has become, pick up a copy of the *Dictionary of Occupational Titles* sometime and leaf through it. It, and books like it, list some 20,000 functions (my favorite is "bung-hole borer") and next to each, a number. The idea with many of these books is for you to look up your job title and, with it, the numbers referencing all the functions for which the government says you'd be qualified. Wonderful. We've reduced ourselves to numbered drones rather than talented individuals.

Performing a function can never, in and of itself, be a goal. Instead we perform functions as a means of achieving a goal. Miami is a goal. Driving cross-country to get there isn't.

I have, on at least three occasions, worked with men who had been the president of the last company they worked for. In each case, they insisted that they wanted only to be president of another company — any company.

Performing a function can never,

in and of itself,

be a goal.

"In that case," I asked them, "you'd be willing to work as president of a company that produces pornographic films?"

Each of them recoiled in shock and answered, "Absolutely not." The point, of course, is that we all have a line below which we will not go and another line above which we'd love to be. Most of us, however, spend our careers as functionaries in the grey area between. Your goals lie above that higher line.

In order to set some goals, you need to "de-program" yourself and get at what you really want, while simultaneously overcoming your fears. Here's how:

Take an honest, objective look at yourself. The more competent people are, the more strongly they identify with their function and the harder it is to take this look. Successful people have the ability to stand outside themselves and accurately judge their strengths and weaknesses. Then they can make valid decisions from within.

Take an objective look at all the different economic enterprises in this country. There are about 25,000 of them. Surely many of them — other than the ones in your current field — have applications for your talents. Don't worry about what you *have* done and don't rule out anything because you don't have experience. Just because you've been working as a widget-washer for the last 15 years doesn't mean you have to do it for the next 15. You may have developed scores of other talents in those 15 years that you can apply elsewhere. I've known countless people who talk themselves out of something because of our society's fetish for "experience."

Look at the market without fear or at least, learn to manage that fear. People back away from things they really want because they're afraid of being hurt by them. Have you ever been afraid of approaching an individual you'd like to know? This same fear of rejection comes into play in career moves. We can get just about anything we want if we are willing to pay the price. Unfortunately, many people develop an irrational fear of the price without ever finding out what the price really is.

Carve out a vision. How would you like everything to turn out in a year? In five, ten or fifteen years? Make your vision attainable — you're not going to play in the NFL if you're 5'2" and weigh 100 pounds — and specific. The goal "to be president of a company" is little more than a pious hope. What kind of company? In what field? How large a company?

Once you've set a goal for yourself, you must determine the methods by which you'll reach it, but that's another subject. **When all is said and done, perhaps the most important step in building the self-confidence necessary to develop professional business relationships, is to have a focus.** Once you have clearly identified your interests and abilities, you have a legitimate basis for building relationships with people with like interests.

If you have honestly identified a field of interest and are pursuing a goal within that field, you will be in a better position to build relationships which develop into new positions and new friendships — the best combination of all.

◆ Self-Employment: When Is It the Right Choice?

There are some people who were simply *meant* to be running their own business. They're the people whose needs for independence and leadership will never be satisfied by working for someone else, no matter how much they like the work or how good they are at it.

Some years ago, a man who had been the pastor of a small church retained my services. He and his wife lived in a church-supplied house on a subsistence income. But he loved caring for his people. He had outstanding talents for diplomacy, tact and administration. He also had a fascination with, and would fantasize about, investments — pretending he had put huge sums into various stocks and bonds, then following their progress in the newspaper.

Eventually, this man got caught in a cross fire between two factions of his congregation and was forced out of his ministry. Not sure what to do with his life, he took a job sitting in one of those little watchtowers on a drawbridge, which left him plenty of time to just think. Can you guess where he wound up?

This man is a perfect example of someone who was right for self-employment. He had the talent, the need, the drive and the clarity of mind to do it right. Anyway, a typical employer would have ignored his talents, looked only at his background as a minister, and laughed him right out the door no matter what kind of job he was looking for.

He and a partner established a financial planning firm. He was perfect for it and the firm has been — and continues to be — extremely successful. It is individuals like this man who establish the 5 to 10 percent of the start-up businesses that succeed each year.

On the other hand, I've worked with a disproportionately high percentage of people who started self-employment ventures and failed (or succeeded and hated it).

Self-employment should be viewed only as a means to an end, with that end being a career goal. If there is a field or industry that you absolutely love and in which you are sure you have the talent to succeed, then self-employment might be the right choice.

The reason is pretty simple. Joe Average gets fired or burned out and decides he's going to start his own business. Not because he's right for it, but because he's too angry or frustrated with "the system" to look for other work. As nearly everyone does at one time or another, Joe hears the call of the wild: Self-employment. It sounds like a fairly attractive choice.

So, Joe establishes Average, Inc. Before long, however, he realizes that self-employment is a 25-hour-a-day, eight-day-a-week commitment. He realizes that he really doesn't have the business acumen to make smart decisions or keep the books, nor does he have the people skills he needs to deal with customers. Within six months, Average, Inc. is out of business and Joe is even angrier and more frustrated than before.

He'll tell everyone (and everyone will tell him) that Average, Inc. was simply undercapitalized. That, so they say, is why most businesses fail.

I can't agree. If the toughness, the business sense, and the people skills were there, the capital would have been there as well.

There are times when self-employment is the right career choice, and that's what it should be — an open choice. Still, I think those times are rare.

What's more, self-employment should never be a goal in itself. If it were, it wouldn't matter whether you owned a restaurant or a ditch-digging business. But it does matter. It matters a great deal.

Self-employment should be viewed only as a means to an end, with that end being a career goal. If there is a field or industry that you absolutely love and in which you're sure you have the talent to succeed, then self-employment might be the right choice. That is, if you can clearly identify strong needs within yourself for independence and leadership.

Even then, I usually urge people to put the idea on a shelf for a little while, to mull it over. It is, after all, like buying a car. It's human nature to convince yourself that you've purchased the best one available, bar none, and ignore the problems. It's not until after you've driven it for awhile that you start to recognize and acknowledge its shortcomings.

Besides, the decision to start your own business is far more serious than the decision to go to work for someone else. You can walk away from a job. It's much more difficult to walk away from your own business.

◆ Assessing the Corporate Personality

Assuming you will not opt for self-employment, the ability to assess and adapt to an employer's personality is, without question, a major element in building a successful career. Too often, perhaps more often than not, when people lose or leave their jobs, it's because of personality conflicts rather than incompetence.

When I talk about an employer's personality, however, I'm not talking only about the manager's personality. I'm talking about the *corporate* personality, something far too many of us overlook in our career decisions.

Corporations, like individual people, have distinct personalities. In fact, when people band together in a group, for whatever reason, the group develops a *group* personality that is quite distinct from the personalities of the individuals. Often the personality differences between groups are easily recognizable. At other times, they are extremely subtle.

Most of us, I think, can easily see the personality differences between Americans as a group and the Japanese as a group. The personality differences between Americans and Canadians, on the other hand, are a bit more difficult to define, but they're clearly there. Similarly, I think most of us could easily see the personality differences between, say, an ad agency and an accounting firm. At the same time there could be subtle, but clearly definable, personality differences between two ad agencies.

**The ideal is to get a clear fix
on a company's personality
before you accept a job,
and accept positions only with those
whose personalities
match your own.**

Corporations are also very much like people in the sense that they're born, go through infancy, childhood, teen years, and adulthood. They become elderly and sometimes die. Corporations are different from individuals, of course, in that they can go through radical personality changes by changing the people in the key decision-making positions. Chrysler is a prime example.

The point is, though, it's generally easy to characterize a corporation in human terms, much as we would characterize ourselves. The key is to develop an honest and objective personality profile of yourself, and then determine whether a potential employer matches that profile.

Some personality traits commonly seen in corporations are:

Open or closed. Some corporations are honest and direct in their dealings with employees, suppliers and customers. Others tend to be defensive, closed to criticism and unwilling to accept the idea that something they're doing is less than perfect.

Flexible or inflexible. Chances are you've worked for a company that was almost militaristic in its approach, expecting people to fall into a routine and adhere to rigid guidelines. Other companies allow broad latitude for their employees and encourage them to take creative liberties with their jobs.

Aggressive or defensive, progressive or conservative (two commonly used adjectives), **outgoing or reserved, formal or informal.** Just as these words are used to describe people, so can they be used to describe corporations.

In career terms, the ideal is to get a clear fix on a company's personality *before* you accept a job with it, and accept positions only with those whose personalities match your own.

This is easier said than done, but here are some hints for doing so:

If possible, talk to several employees within the company. The interview process usually involves just one person in the corporation, so bear in mind that this one person does not reflect the corporate personality.

Assess the personality of the CEO and his or her immediate subordinates. They probably set the tone for the company as a whole. If you're interviewing with the CEO, bear in mind that he or she may be insulated from how others perceive the company due to the natural tendency of employees to cater to their boss. For example, a CEO may feel that his company is a good listener because his people all listen to him, while the company might be perceived by the rest of the world as a good talker but a poor listener.

If the company has branch offices, visit them and see what they're like. How do people answer the phones? How do they address each other? How are the offices decorated?

All corporations, by virtue of the fact that they are corporations, have some structure, just as all people, by virtue of the fact that they are people, have arms and legs. The important question is how they use that structure and whether you can function comfortably within it.

Again, I can't emphasize enough the importance of getting a fix on a corporation's personality *before* you take a job with it. And don't ever accept a position with the expectation that either your personality, or the corporation's personality, will change. That's a certain step toward career unhappiness.

◆ Improving Your Career Without Change

Usually, when people think about making a career move, they think in terms of moving to another company or perhaps into an entirely different field. In fact, most of the people I've worked with over the years have made exactly that kind of move.

But it's also possible to improve your career without making such a dramatic move, by moving within your current company. After all, you're already intimately familiar with the company and (hopefully) you enjoy a mutual respect and close working relationship with the employer (your boss) — items essential for any successful career move. Besides, a move within a company is far less traumatic than making a complete change.

People often find themselves at a dead end (see Chapter Seven) and automatically assume that the solution is to make a drastic move. Rarely, however, do they look at their current company to see what else they might do *without* moving.

I once worked with a woman who had risen, over the course of ten years, from secretary to operations manager at a large brokerage house, the highest level she could expect to attain along her career path. She initially assumed she would have to move to a new field. However, she went on to realize that she had an untapped sales ability. Therefore, rather than leave her company, she carefully negotiated a move into the sales division of the firm. That was many years ago. At this writing more than 20 years later, she is still with the same firm and is one of it's two top sales producers.

**To make a positive career movement
within your own company
often requires developing
a more realistic picture of yourself —
in your own mind
and in the mind
of your employer.**

Much of what's involved in making this kind of career improvement (essentially creating your own promotion) relates to the fundamentals discussed in earlier chapters: Identifying your internal talents; identifying your internal needs; setting goals; and being completely objective about yourself, your future and your company. Then you must market (communicate) yourself and your talents to your employer.

One major problem you may encounter is that while you've grown and matured in your job, your employer may well perceive you as being the same person you were when you started. The woman I mentioned earlier was still perceived by many people in the brokerage house as being "just a secretary." This was one of the biggest obstacles she had to overcome. The challenge, then, is to develop in the mind of your boss a more realistic picture of yourself.

That's not easy. It requires an extraordinary amount of tact and diplomacy. If handled improperly, it can inalterably change your relationship with your employer for the worse. You can't just walk in and demand a change or lecture the boss about how the company can be improved. That's a one-way ticket to the unemployment line. At the same time, it is necessary to be direct about what you think you can do and how you can help the company. As I said, it's not easy.

While a step by step how-to guide is not possible, here are a few suggestions:

Once you've determined that a career improvement within the company is in order, and you've determined how to market your talents, ask your boss for a confidential meeting. During this meeting, don't ask for action and don't get confrontational. Keep it friendly and help your boss think out loud about his or her daily responsibilities and plans for the company's future. Most employers will be happy to discuss such things.

Listen carefully and demonstrate a sincere interest in what he or she is saying (without appearing to be a bootlicker). If you can't do this much, perhaps it really is time for you to move on to another company.

If, on the other hand, you truly believe you can address the boss' concerns, he or she will surely want to know about it. Again, make suggestions, not demands. Virtually all bosses like to think that they initiated good ideas (like moving you to another position in the company) and as I've said before, people who feel that we've listened to them will give us anything we want.

As much as anything, it's a matter of making a *decision*. If you've developed the self-sufficiency and complete open-mindedness about your talents, needs, and goals, any decision you make, and that you help others make, will be the best one.

◆ Making a Promotion Work

The Peter Principle suggests that we each rise to the level of our incompetence. The idea has been widely accepted — probably prompted by the fact that almost everyone stumbles a bit after being promoted to a new level of responsibility. Unfortunately, the "stumbles" frequently have a snowballing effect. The promoted individual either never achieves a peak of efficiency, or loses efficiency and leaves.

My experience suggests that in most cases, this does not have to be. I have seen managers reach their "level of incompetence," rethink the situation, then negotiate a new position which carries them beyond where they were. When someone is to be promoted, I think it is incumbent on two people to safeguard against the Peter Principle: The person to be promoted, and the manager who is offering the promotion. Let's look at the subject from the viewpoint of the person to be promoted. (The employer's perspective is discussed elsewhere.)

When the boss offers us a promotion, an ingrained reaction causes most of us to snap to, say "Yes, sir," and accept.

There is something of an ego reaction in it: Our work has finally been recognized, and besides that, we'll get more money. And we quiet the stab of fear within us by telling ourselves that the boss must be right or he wouldn't have offered the promotion.

After all, he knows us and the company so well. (I recall a client who expressed disbelief at the thought that his former boss, the president of a company, could possibly suffer from the common human problems of stress, fear, anxiety, and lack of objectivity.)

**When someone is to be promoted,
it is incumbent on two people
to guard against the Peter Principle:
The person to be promoted, and the manager
who offers the promotion.**

If you have been offered a promotion, you should, as objectively as possible, answer a number of pertinent questions:

Is the promotion within the scope of *your own* career objectives? If it is, fine; proceed to the next question. If it is not, then isn't it time to determine what your next step should be? Can the promotion serve as a temporary stepping stone to the next valid career level, or would it be a setback?

Are you ready for the promotion, and do you have the necessary talent and experience to handle the new responsibilities effectively? If yes, go to the next question. If not, it would be unwise to accept the promotion. If you are uncertain, then it would be a good idea to retain professional help, or (in special circumstances) discuss the matter openly with the boss in order to settle your mind. It would be a shame to refuse a promotion simply out of fear. Oftentimes it can be enough to have a clear description of the new responsibilities by the boss, to discuss those responsibilities with the outgoing manager, and to have some talks with members of that department.

Does the promotion include all the elements necessary to meet your and the company's (employer's) needs? What is the nature of the new responsibilities, and will you have the requisite authority to fulfill them? Or will you be required to seek approval even for less important matters? What problems did your predecessor have, and how can you be sure that you will not have the same ones? Do you have the authority (and the budget) to hire necessary personnel and to terminate those who are not doing their jobs? Is the salary and other compensation appropriate to the level of your responsibility and the contribution you will make? Even if it is, should you not (professionally) negotiate for additional compensation?

What kind of training or other preparation can the employer provide to accelerate your adjustment to your new responsibilities? Is there a specific kind of help you can request? Have you given thought to the habit patterns you have developed in previous jobs and how they might make your transition more difficult? Have you thought about the new relationships you will have, both with the people you have known and with new subordinates? How will you deal with those who, for years, have been co-workers and friends? (So often friendships are strained and even destroyed when someone is promoted. Sadly, in most cases it need not have happened had there been sufficient prior reflection and effective communication.)

What about your management style in the new position? Good communication skills will make the transition easier. No matter how competent, any newly promoted manager has lots to learn about how things work in the new position. A savvy manager candidly admits that he or she is in a learning mode and then seeks out each subordinate individually to ask for suggestions. Our experience shows that very few bosses do this. Instead, they tend to immediately start making changes and issuing orders, alienating subordinates in the process.

Perhaps it can be a consolation to many to say that nearly 100 percent of newly promoted employees stumble to some degree. Minor stumbles are usually covered up, and the person grows into his or her new responsibilities, over time developing a style that is appropriate for the new position. But all too often, a newly promoted person stumbles so badly or so frequently that the repercussions are more serious — demotion or even losing the job. When we effectively learn to take charge of our own careers, we will take the positive steps required to ensure that this will not happen.

> In this great land
> whose freedom the people of the world
> yearn for and strive to emulate,
> one important freedom remains to be achieved:
> The freedom to choose our careers
> based on our personal talents and desires,
> rather than on governmental, educational,
> social and familial persuasion.

"I want to thank you for the renewed strength and faith in myself that you have helped me to re-acquire ..."

D. B., Client

CHAPTER SIX

The Ultimate Challenge: Tell Them Who You Are And What You Can Do

*Perhaps the greatest challenge
in business relationships
is learning to establish and maintain
effective boss-to-subordinate relationships.*

♦ Communicating Yourself

"Communication" has become something of a pervasive catch-word in today's business world. Those who do the best job at "communication" are those who will be the most successful, we are told.

Properly understood, this is absolutely true, not just for corporations, but for individuals as well. Communication in all its forms is the basis of all interpersonal dynamics. And yet, for all the books, seminars and courses in communication, we as a society seem to do a terrible job of communicating our true selves to others.

There are several reasons for this, not the least of which is that no two people seem to have the same definition of "communication." One thing is certain, though: In career terms, sitting across a desk from a potential employer and reciting where you worked and when you worked there is *not* communication, nor is allowing the employer you work for to develop a static, stereo-typed image of who you are and what you can do.

The business world, and personnel departments especially and understandably, have unfortunately propagated the myth that you are what you have been. In essence, they're saying, "Tell me what you've done up until now, and then I'll decide whether I want you or want to keep you." People who choose to buck the system are frequently punished by being passed over for jobs or having their resumes ignored, even though they may very well be the most qualified people. (And I still encourage people to buck the system in a professional manner.)

There are three basic types of communication: First is **verbal communication,** or communicating through words. It means being able to formulate sentences so others can understand our ideas, and to understand others when they do the same. Some studies suggest that a small percentage of what we learn from each other actually comes from words.

Next is **"empathetic" communication,** in other words, using body language (posture, behavior, tone of voice, etc.), to project and receive huge paragraphs of meaning. Studies suggest that more than 50 percent, even up to 90 percent, of communication comes from this level.

Lastly is self-knowledge, or self-awareness, leading to **"self-communication."** This is what successful job seekers must master if they are to take charge of their careers.

Self-Communication:
Expressing from one person to another
the true essence
of the most abstract and
complex subject on Earth: A human being.

Self-communication involves active listening, along with strong verbal skills and a heavy dose of self-honesty. It is the foundation of all human communication.

As with all other subjects, to successfully communicate your true self, you must:

Understand the subject matter as thoroughly as possible.

Focus on the audience which can benefit from the subject.

Develop an effective method that allows the audience to perceive the benefits.

A good share of the problem is that dealing with self is not like dealing with washing machines, nor like teaching a subject in a classroom. You are communicating the true essence of the most complex and abstract product (subject) on Earth: A human being. And while you must mechanically know how to teach and to sell (two skills that can be easily learned), you must also learn how to present your talents, needs and strengths accurately, honestly and fearlessly.

More commonly, however, people try to gauge what an employer wants to hear and then say it. Not only is this poor communication, it's usually a dead end. The best, most professional communicators are those who can allow their strengths and personality to show through without appearing boastful and who, rather than saying what someone wants to hear, devote more effort to finding people (i.e., potential employers) who will be receptive to what they have to say.

This is not to suggest that you ignore the needs of a potential employer, but rather that you find areas of agreement and focus your communication efforts on those areas. Here in a nutshell, then, is what you need to remember to be effective at communicating your true self:

1. Concentrate on the three fundamentals outlined above.

2. Communicate what you *are* rather than what you *do*.

3. Find areas of agreement and focus on them.

4. Ask questions and listen.

To a great extent, the business world discourages this kind of communication, but you should not get discouraged. You must continue to work at self-honesty and at letting people see your true self.

◆ How to Talk to a Prospective Boss

Perhaps the greatest challenge in business relationships is learning to establish and maintain effective boss-to-subordinate relationships.

There's a common myth in business that employers prefer employees who flatter them, who are subservient. On the contrary, most bosses hire people who have enough confidence and self-esteem that they can establish a relationship of mutual respect.

Of course, it's often difficult to maintain an attitude of respectful equality as a candidate for a career position. When faced with a pair of seemingly cold, beady eyes across a large desk and asked to explain why you deserve a job, it's easy to forget that bosses are human, too.

So how do you hang onto your sense of self-worth and establish a relationship of mutual respect from the beginning? Here are a few suggestions:

Avoid the traditional across-the-desk, resume-based interview. Most of these interviews focus on historical credentials, such as past employment and education, rather than abilities. Instead, concentrate on exploring with a prospective employer ways in which you both might benefit from working together.

Understand the psychological forces affecting the prospective employer. He or she doesn't want to commit to anything that might jeopardize his or her position. This is why as many as 90 percent of open positions are filled through private contacts. It's easier for a boss to take a chance on someone whom he or she meets through a friend than to hire a stranger off the street. Once you understand this, you can focus on becoming better known and thus, be seen as an attractive candidate.

Remember that the prospective employer fears rejection, too. Surprisingly, I've found that an employer may be very interested after the first interview, but will hesitate to call the candidate again for fear that he or she has already accepted a position with another employer. Rejection is especially difficult for the employer when he or she begins to think that you are the right person for the job. That's why you must be the one to keep in contact.

Expect to spend time developing a relationship. Don't expect to really get to know a prospective boss in the first half-hour interview ... or the second ... or even the third. It takes repeated contact to really begin to build trust and respect.

Realize that employers often deliberately refrain from showing enthusiasm for any one candidate. As many as 50 people may be interviewed for a single job. Knowing that 49 of those candidates will be rejected often makes an employer defensive and embarrassed. He or she tries to avoid encouraging any of them so that final rejection will be easier.

Bosses want to be listened to and to be *understood*. Very few people ever stop to think about the stress and anxiety experienced by bosses. Several executives with responsibility for hundreds of people have confided to me that they sometimes wake up in the middle of the night worrying about what will happen if no one shows up for work the next day. Because these kinds of worries often seem silly to subordinates who perceive bosses as "having it made," subordinates overlook opportunities to understand how they fit into the boss's concerns and overall vision of the business.

Understand that 75 to 80 percent of hiring decisions are based on personality. That's difficult for many candidates to accept and it's almost impossible for most employers to admit. Bosses

---

Expect to spend time developing a relationship.
Remember that a prospective employer
can also fear rejection.
Very few people stop to think about the stress and
anxiety experienced by bosses.

---

do not like to appear irrational, and candidates don't like to admit that their long list of qualifications may not matter. It's easier for both sides to point to lack of education, too little experience, too much experience, salary demands that are too high, etc.

Go beyond the overworked, superficial concept of networking and informational interviewing. In pursuing our career plans, we all need to develop the ability to establish beneficial social and business relationships. However, it's important that these relationships be based on sincere interest in the individual, not on the need to find a job.

**Most employers
do not know how
to conduct an interview.**

◆ How to Conduct a Good Interview

"Well," says the hapless interviewer, staring across the desk at the job seeker, "tell me a little about yourself."

"Okay," responds the nervous applicant. "I was born in Normaltown, Iowa. I graduated from Normal University. And for the last ten years, I've been a widget-washer at Normal, Inc."

So begins the typical job interview — an awkward dance between a decision maker who doesn't know what questions to ask and a job seeker who has no idea how to answer.

But, when you take charge of your career, the interview is a powerful tool that's used to great advantage. It's used to market talents and skills to a potential employer and to gather information: Is this my kind of company? My kind of people? My kind of ethics? My kind of workplace?

Unfortunately, most people go into an interview with hat in hand, begging for a job, and make three mistakes:

1. They speak enthusiastically about their backgrounds. After awhile, it all sounds the same to an employer. The decision makers are looking for the people who will solve their problems, not those who had the most impressive titles.

2. They talk too much. It's an unerring way to bore an employer and make him or her feel that you're not really interested in the company. Ask questions. It's the only way to show interest. Relate the questions to the anxieties and daily concerns of the employer.

3. They don't know how to listen. Too many people go into an interview having already decided what they're going to say and what they hope to find. As a result, they fail to perceive the real needs and concerns of the employer. Those who do perceive the real needs and concerns, however, can put themselves in a position to show how they can fill them.

In another publication, we give step-by-step instructions on how to be a good interviewee. Everyone, however, should develop his or her own style. Some people can come on strong without being intimidating. Others can project strength by being low key. Only you can determine what's best, but here are a few things to remember:

Most employers don't know how to conduct an interview. When they ask open-ended or irrelevant questions (as they invariably will), use them as an opportunity to discuss the benefits you and you alone can offer.

Do a little research and learn something about the company before you go into the interview. If you're asked, "What do you know about our firm?" and you answer "Nothing," the interview will, for all intents and purposes, be over.

Treat the employer as an authority figure but establish respectful equality. People who grovel do not get hired. Remember that employers are human, have egos and are under tremendous pressure to hire the right person. Ask them about their own abilities and responsibilities. It helps put them at ease.

(One of my former clients starts his interviews by asking, "What do you as an executive feel is the major concern of the executive in the business world today?" The question strokes the interviewer's ego by establishing him as an authority on executive problems and, since the answer will be based on his experience within the company, it provides clues to the needs and concerns of the company.)

**The typical job interview is an awkward dance
between a decision maker who doesn't know
what questions to ask
and a job seeker
who has no idea how to answer.**

Begin the interview with a clear statement of why you're there. Interviews are won or lost in the first 30 to 60 seconds, so it's important to establish the fact that you have a purpose in mind, not that you're just looking for a job.

Ask questions that lower barriers and establish rapport (the respectful equality referred to earlier). A fundamental goal in every interview should be to help the employer think out loud. If they're approached in the right way, decision makers will be happy to do so.

Ask for referrals. You can't do this if you're one of ten candidates for an advertised position, but you can if you're approaching decision makers directly.

Establish a reason for getting back to the person to whom you've been talking. Nobody makes a hiring decision on the basis of one interview.

Most important of all: Stay in control of the interview. Keep the conversation focused on the employer's needs and concerns and how you are uniquely qualified to fill them.

Again, none of this is cast in stone. Interviews are impacted by individual style and personality as much as, or more than, any other aspect of taking charge of your career. The important thing is to be *comfortable* in the interview setting. It is essential that you know what you're doing and be confident that you know how to do it. Find out what works best for you and start using interviews to your advantage.

♦ Women in Business

Women in the business world have the deck stacked against them. That's long been true, but I believe it's not nearly as much a factor now as it was ten years ago. The individual woman, with courage and career goals in hand, can overcome the problem. I have worked with a very high number of such women and have watched with intense satisfaction as they have achieved their goals as effectively as men. Freedom of choice and professionalism are, as always, the answer.

There is no question that there are forces in our society working against women from the time they're born until the day they die. But ultimately, all of us are responsible for the success (or lack thereof) we achieve in our own careers. We cannot lean on societal forces as an excuse for failure, because then those forces indeed become a barrier.

People — not just women — are discriminated against on a regular basis. Regardless of what the law says, people are discriminated against because of age, race, gender, education and experience. When people move to a new part of the country, they are not always quickly accepted. Successful people, however, rise above such discrimination.

The American workplace is changing, and women's roles in it are largely responsible for many of the changes. When I first started in career consulting in 1972, very few of my clients were women. It wasn't until the mid '70s that I started working with a significant number of women clients, and even then, most were homemakers looking to reenter the job market. Those who weren't homemakers were secretaries who realized they had greater talents, and nurses or teachers, who wanted to move into another field.

Although we've made great strides, our society still perceives women in many traditional roles. And at the same time, an opposite kind of pressure on women has also emerged — one based on rejecting traditional gender-based values learned early in life. As a result, there is a conflict and an unconscious kind of confusion which makes personal life and career decisions extremely difficult for many women. (I find, however, that an increasing number of younger women have grown up with and are comfortable with the idea that they can do anything they choose.)

The solution, of course, is for each individual to freely and independently establish her own set of values and her career pattern within that framework. Everybody must learn to make career decisions irrespective of pressures. Granted, this may be especially difficult given pressures facing women, but it is by no means impossible.

**The toughness required for success
in the business world
is at least as common among women
as it is among men.
However, it has often been suppressed by women
because of childhood messages
that it is incompatible with femininity.**

First, women must deal openly and honestly with their self-image if they are to have true freedom of choice. As young girls, many women were taught to be dainty and reserved, and this sort of self-image has been carried into womanhood. However, a certain toughness is needed to succeed in the business world, whether or not it is dominated by men. That kind of toughness is as common among women as it is among men, but it has often been suppressed because of the societal pressures already outlined. I once worked with a teacher whose self-image was low because she realized that she was very different from other teachers. She was a very aggressive person, but could not acknowledge that. She offended her fellow teachers. Had she acknowledged her aggressiveness, she could have controlled this personality trait and used it to her advantage.

Second, women must build their careers around *complete professionalism.* It's the surest way to defuse the threat many men feel from powerful women. Unfortunately, many women who attain positions of authority, feel the need to "prove" themselves and rely on intimidation rather than cooperation. This is a major mistake. Women (men, too, for that matter) can capitalize on the fact that men and women naturally like each other. Women who can take an easy, professional approach within the lines of authority will be readily accepted. (And here's some food for thought: I've often heard from my female clients that the people with whom they have the most trouble are other women. I'm not sure why this is so.)

Finally, as I said at the outset, women must realize that they and they alone as individuals are ultimately responsible for their own success. They must clearly identify their internal talents and requirements, set goals for themselves and take the necessary steps to take charge of their careers.

Men and women can and must complement each other in the business world just as they do in life. Yes, there are some antiquated attitudes and terrible societal pressures, but it's professionalism and self-assurance, not demands and lectures, that will change them. The idea that women in the business world have the deck stacked against them is true, but it's never stacked against the competent, professional individual.

◆ Negotiating Your True Worth

Say the word "negotiation" and you probably think of a U.S. secretary of state and a foreign minister from the Mid-East, the Orient, or Europe squaring off across a table. Perhaps you think of union leaders and management poring over a contract. While this sort of bargaining on behalf of others is a common form of negotiation, the fact is that virtually every form of human contact is a negotiation of some kind. And while most people are comfortable negotiating on behalf of others, few ever develop the skill and strength needed to negotiate for themselves.

Negotiation, as I use it here, is not so much a bargaining process as it is an effort to find a mutuality between two people with compatible goals.

This is especially true if you're seeking to take charge of your career. First you must negotiate within an entire field, identifying the companies for which you'd be willing to work. Then you must negotiate with individual companies and finally with an individual employer. And remember: Negotiation begins long before an employer makes an offer.

"But wait," you're thinking. "In order to negotiate I have to be in a position of strength."

That's very true. And if you conduct your career moves in a directed and professional manner you *will* be in a position of strength. It's the strength that comes from having a purpose and a mission. The strength that comes from within.

I know that may sound like so much psychobabble, but look at it this way: If you were approached by a salesman who begged and pleaded with you to buy something you didn't need, would he be able to get his asking price from you? Of course not. Or, if a commodity is too available, what happens? The price comes down and the buying public loses interest.

This is typically what happens as people move along their career paths. They plead for jobs (at least implicitly) and make themselves too available. They put themselves in a position of weakness.

What, then, to do about it?

First, go into every interview with the notion that you may or may not want to work at this place. You're shopping for an employer, not begging for a job.

Second, anytime you're offered anything, appreciate it *highly.* But don't immediately accept it. That's your cue to start some heavy-duty negotiating.

Finally, you must exude confidence from every pore, every molecule in your body. Everyone responds to confident people. You can't control your technical competence or years of experience, but you can control your attitude. Make sure it's good.

Eventually, of course, you'll get an offer from an employer. When that happens, your relationship swings a complete 180 degrees. The employer has decided that he or she wants to buy and will try to close the deal at the lowest price possible. You are suddenly in your position of greatest strength.

At this point, it's helpful to remember a few rules:

When you receive an offer — direct or implicit — the employer becomes the seller, and you become the buyer. And this puts you in a position of real power.

Avoid talking about money until there has been an adequate presentation of exactly what the job entails and you're sure this is what you want. Money will stifle further conversation.

Never accept an offer during a first interview. First-interview offers are often a sign of desperation.

If an employer makes an offer during a later interview, neither accept nor reject it. Negotiate. If it's a lowball offer, either come back with a higher figure or change the subject. If it's higher than you expected, keep a straight face and ask for more. Don't worry — the employer has his mind made up that you're what he wants and no employer will name the highest figure the first time around.

Always have the employer name a figure first. Then name a higher figure from which you're willing to come down.

Be sure your compensation is based on your real value to the employer. If you work for less than you are worth, it's the start of your demise. You're likely to be unhappy and your employer will either lose respect for you because you accepted less or feel guilty because he got away with it.

Don't make demands. Be professional, respectful and courteous. As I said earlier, show your appreciation for every offer.

Don't accept someone's word or handshake. Get it in writing.

The notion of a job seeker not immediately and gratefully accepting an offer is probably foreign to most people. But face it — offers are not made lightly and aren't going to be withdrawn just because you ask for more. Ask. You'll be glad you did.

"Your advice on salary and benefits negotiations was powerful and effective. I've doubled my salary to nearly six figures, and am receiving additional bonuses, retirement funds, company stock, more vacation, a company car and several other benefits. I had to keep my composure when their offer was much higher than my expectations; then I asked for more and got it!"

D. M., Client

"[I] have enough confidence in myself to be honest about my feelings and needs while in an interview. I didn't say things just because I thought it was what they wanted to hear ... I may have turned some companies off, but the ones I turned on, I turned on because of me. That sure feels good."

K. G., Client

CHAPTER SEVEN

Coping With Difficult Situations

*The great strength of humor
is that it allows us
to tell the truth about ourselves
and our emotions
in a socially acceptable way.*

◆ Why Everyone Should Cultivate a Sense of Humor

One of the best tools for building good working relationships is a sense of humor.

Not only does the right kind of humor make work more fun, but it provides an acceptable method for expressing emotion. A bit of gentle humor can defuse a tense situation, help someone else see your point of view, or make a point that might otherwise provoke hostility.

A sense of humor helped one man I know get a job. Bill was being interviewed by three vice presidents from a dairy company. The interview was not going well; the three men seemed cold and unresponsive. Then one of the interviewers asked my friend how he got into the dairy field. He replied, "because I have warm hands." Everyone laughed, the atmosphere relaxed, and Bill ended up getting the job. Within six months he had a raise and a promotion.

This illustrates the greatest strength of humor: It allows us to tell the truth about ourselves and our emotions in a socially acceptable way. Chances are very good that Bill had not planned to work in a dairy. The person who plans from childhood to embark on a particular career and then does it, is very rare. Most of us fall into our careers because of luck, accident or family circumstances.

With a light touch, this man referred to that underlying social truth, tapped a responsive chord, and spoke volumes about the kind of person he is.

The interesting thing about humor is that humorous people, perhaps without exception, are strong people. They are aware of their strengths and weaknesses, and they are not afraid to admit that they don't know everything. They are willing to poke fun at themselves.

Of course, humor is a very personal thing. To use a sense of humor effectively, every person has to determine what works for him or her. For example, some people can tell a joke and have everyone laughing. Another person can tell the same joke and get no reaction at all. Humor can't be forced and it can't be faked. But it can be learned. Most professional comedians say they learned to be funny by studying people's reactions, being sensitive to their audience, and developing a sense of timing.

Humorous people, perhaps without exception, are strong people. And there seems to be a close connection between humor and attentiveness to other people's needs.

Because humor is so personal there is always a risk in using it, but there are some general guidelines:

Certainly, off-color, sexist and racist jokes, and jokes that belittle or insult another person, should always be avoided.

It's also wise to remember that people from other cultures have very different forms of humor. Anyone who has traveled can vouch for the fact that what sets people howling with laughter in England may not do a thing for someone in Japan. So it's best to be very cautious about using American humor when meeting with business people from other countries. If you are not familiar with that culture's humor, at best, a joke will fall flat; at worst, it will offend.

The best humor is spontaneous — or it seems spontaneous. By thinking about a situation and running through possible scenarios, it is possible to develop humorous responses that are easy to use if the opportunity arises.

Appropriate humor certainly has a place in the workplace. There seems to be a close connection between humor and attentiveness to people's needs. A happy office is easy to spot because there is a certain amount of easy banter that goes on. The employees use humor to empathize with each other, and to share each other's achievements and disappointments.

It's too bad that more workplaces don't benefit from humor. Sometimes we get so caught up in the stresses of getting the job done that we lose sight of the humor in a situation. I'm not suggesting that American businesses should be run by a bunch of clowns. Humor can be carried too far. But it also has a legitimate function as a powerful business tool.

Having said that, here's one of my favorite jokes:

A woman was invited as a guest to a jokester's club. During the course of the meeting members would stand up and recite a number — like "169" — and the rest of the club members would roar with laughter.

Intrigued, the woman leaned over to her host and asked, "What is this? Why are people laughing at a number?"

Her host explained that the club members had memorized thousands of jokes, so just hearing the number of the joke made them remember it and start laughing.

The woman was enthralled with this and asked her host to give her the number of a good joke. The host did and she stood up at the first opportunity and said, "98". There was dead silence.

The woman turned to her friend and asked, "What's the matter?" Did you give me a bad joke?"

Her host shook his head and said, "Some people just can't tell a joke."

Unfortunately, learning to use humor effectively isn't as easy as memorizing a few numbers. But it can be done, and it is worth the effort. A sense of humor at the right place and time can be a real boon to your career.

◆ Dealing with a Problem Boss

"I just couldn't get along with my boss."

How many times have you heard someone give that (or something unprintable) as their reason for leaving a job? I know that I, in my capacity as a career consultant, have heard it hundreds of times.

Dealing with a problem boss can be as gut-wrenching as trying to patch up a shaky marriage, maybe tougher. There are, after all, powerful emotions involved in the boss/employee relationship that can create overwhelming barriers to communication. I find, however, that those who can rise above it are those with the most successful careers.

Now, let me say up front that it's easy to be a bad boss and most bosses who become problems for their employees don't do so intentionally. It's important to keep this in mind when dealing with a problem boss. Still, these things must be dealt with.

The things that make a boss problematic run the gamut of possibilities. Let's look at a few of them, along with some suggestions for how you might deal with them:

1. The failure to acknowledge talent, ability or successes, and the tendency to horde all the credit. This is without a doubt the most common problem and the easiest one to correct. A boss who fails to give you your due is probably suffering from a lack of confidence or some kind of anxiety over his or her own position.

As a subordinate you can ease those anxieties by offering your boss praise for a job well done. Remember, a boss hears every problem and complaint, but rarely hears any praise. And I think it's a universal truism that if you give praise you get praise. When a boss hears from subordinates that they think he or she is doing a good job, he's likely to say the same of them.

**The most common failures of bosses
are the failure to acknowledge talent,
ability and successes,
and the tendency
to horde all the credit.**

---

2. The failure to give guidance. This also commonly results from a lack of confidence, but it could also be laziness, ineptitude or a desire to be perceived as a nice guy. Of course, many people prefer to work in an atmosphere in which they have broad latitude. More often, however, people begin stepping on each other's toes and become unproductive. Direct communication with your boss is the only answer. He or she needs to know how you feel. If the problem is that your boss has been given accountability and responsibility but no authority by his higher-ups, perhaps it's up to the employees to take their case directly to those higher-ups.

3. The over-application of authority. You know, the dictator syndrome. There are a number of very successful companies in which the CEO wields absolute authority, and I guess you can't knock this approach if it works. In the case where the owner of the company rules with an iron fist, you simply need to decide whether you want to stay and live with it or move on to something else. I don't think there's much you can do about it. At the department-head level, though, you need to make a decision as to whether such dictatorial behavior is changeable. If it is, direct communication is the answer. You need to tactfully explain to your boss that you could be more productive if you had more leeway.

The key is to clearly show your boss how he or she, or the company, would benefit by a change in behavior.

4. The failure to make good or timely decisions. Again, there's not much you can do about this, and again, you have to make a decision as to whether or not you're willing to live with it. In some cases, it might be possible to tactfully question the rationale behind some decisions and in this way help your boss see "the error of his ways."

5. The failure to listen or give subordinates any platform for providing input. This is the most difficult problem to deal with, but also the one that is most immediately solvable. You simply need to steel yourself and ask that your boss start listening to his or her subordinates. If you get a negative response, I recommend that you get yourself out of that situation as soon as possible. Listening is the key and most basic activity in all human relationships. A boss who does not, or will not, listen will rob you of your self-respect.

Some people go along for years with the knowledge that they are never going to get along with their boss. But they ignore it so they can hang on to the facade of security that comes with a paycheck. These people are hardly what I would call successful. Successful people take matters in hand and endeavor to change them.

♦ Dealing with the Impossible Relationship

No matter how astute you are at observing and fostering business relationships, there's always the chance that a relationship will begin to go sour without any apparent reason or warning.

Usually relationships sour because one of the people involved suddenly becomes fearful or uneasy. Fear or unease may be the result of some kind of emotional aberration, a personal problem, or pressure from employers.

A good example of this is the case of two men who worked together and had been firm friends for 15 years. They lived on the same street and their families socialized regularly. One day a vice president at their company offered the younger man a promotion which the older man had been promised. The younger man accepted the position and abruptly stopped speaking to the older man.

Their friendship, which had been built over 15 years of working and playing together, ended overnight.

A similar thing happened to a woman who was in upper management at her company. For years she had received excellent reviews from her bosses. She had advanced steadily through the company and had recently been one of two finalists for a much higher position.

One morning she was called into a vice president's office and asked to resign. She was never told what happened. She assumed that the woman who was promoted instead of her didn't want her to remain and exercised her new political clout to have her ousted.

Then there was the man who had been a partner in a very profitable business for many years. He and his partner worked well together, the business was growing and he enjoyed his work — until the day he showed up at work and discovered that the entire business, through a legal maneuver, had been pulled out from under him by his trusted partner.

These situations are repeated many times in business. Every indication is that a relationship is built on mutual trust and respect, and suddenly, a colleague, friend or client turns on you.

The best way to prepare for, and deal with, these situations is to balance being nice with being watchful. We should do everything we can to foster good human relationships while recognizing that humans have frailties and weaknesses which can sabotage good relationships very quickly.

When a relationship has been damaged by deceit or maliciousness, there are two methods of dealing with the situation:

One is to recognize the problem and get out of it as quickly as possible. The other is to fight.

Whether you choose to leave or fight depends on several factors:

The circumstances. If you have been fired abruptly, your ability to fight may be limited to the courts. Although you may be in the right, bringing a case to court can severely limit your chances of finding a new job — and, as a lawyer friend once told me, in most cases only the lawyers win financially.

On the other hand, if you are simply involved in some particularly malicious office politics, and you love a good fight and believe you can win, fighting may be your best option.

Your responsibilities. Single people with few responsibilities beyond themselves often find it easier to fight than do people who are married and have a family to support.

The company. In some companies, political infighting is expected. The person who is a skilled politician is a highly valued employee. Other companies discourage competition among employees and consider those who fight to be troublemakers.

Although these situations usually cannot be avoided, there are steps you can take to limit your chances of being involved in one.

Perhaps the most important step is to avoid going into business with close friends or family members. There are, of course, many examples of families and friends who started small businesses and became multi-millionaires. However, a large number of these businesses fail, and the friendships are destroyed.

Another step is to avoid becoming overly chummy with co-workers. Personal relationships and business relationships are different, and it's rare that they are combined successfully. At some point, people who have drifted into very personal relationships with co-workers realize that the working relationship and the personal relationship might conflict. One or both try to pull back from the relationship and, in the process, hurt each other.

A third step is without fail to observe the legalities of a working relationship. Be sure that business relationships are clearly spelled out in contracts.

It's important to realize that these situations are almost never caused by something we've done; often times they are beyond our control. The best defense of all is to conduct ourselves professionally at all times, and to combine trust with the safeguards necessary to maintain a good relationship.

◆ What to Do When Your Mentor Turns on You

"Find a mentor" is advice frequently given to individuals who want to get ahead in their careers. The idea is that a mentor will serve as teacher, promoter, advisor and sounding board. Such a relationship should be cultivated carefully.

All truly professional people have mentors, or "coaches," who provide support, training and objective feedback.
Such a relationship should be cultivated carefully —
and terminated when it is no longer beneficial to both.

But there may come a time when the mentor relationship becomes a negative factor instead of a positive one.

For example, I recently spoke with a man who had been working with a mentor who seemed very supportive. The mentor was a top executive within the company and seemed to be grooming this man for advancement to upper management. But suddenly the relationship began to change. The executive began to criticize this man's performance. Previously his actions and decisions had been praised, but now they were corrected or overridden. This man was confused and hurt. Later, after he had left the company, he discovered that this was a typical scenario. The executive had had a series of protégés, all of whom were "golden boys" for awhile and then, for no clear reason, fell into disfavor and subsequently left the company.

This situation is a common one — more common than most people suspect. Mentors may turn against their protégés for several reasons. One is that they may suddenly realize that they have created their own competition. By teaching and guiding a promising employee, they often groom a viable replacement for themselves when they have no intention of moving on. When it becomes apparent that the subordinate is ready for bigger and better things, the mentor may become fearful of losing his or her job. Since the mentor is almost always more powerful, the protégé ends up leaving the company or transferring to another department.

Another, and I believe at least equally common, occurrence is for protégés to become "chesty" and give every evidence that they believe they know more and are more capable than their mentors. This is a particularly bitter pill for the mentor who has put so much effort and so many hopes into the grooming of the subordinate.

A third reason is that a mentor may expect a protégé to develop certain talents or abilities, but finds that the protégé never lives up to expectations. Some protégés become so dependent on their mentors that they never develop their own initiative within the job responsibility. A good example of this is the individual who was told by her mentor, "You will never get a raise unless you ask for one," and yet never asked for a raise.

Another reason is that a wise mentor may realize that the relationship is no longer beneficial. Both mentor and protégé may be ready to move on to new responsibilities. This is similar to what happens between athletes and good coaches. There are many stories about Olympic-class athletes who start out with a coach and then after several years are told, "I have done all I can for you ... you need a new coach."

Finally, the relationship between a mentor and a protégé may deteriorate because, although the mentor has an intellectual desire to see the protégé succeed, there is an emotional reluctance to risk having the protégé become visibly more competent.

None of this is to say that having a mentor is a bad idea. But if you are considering entering such a relationship — whether as the mentor or the protégé — identify your motives and expectations and understand the potential risks.

The biggest risk is the tendency for the protégé to believe that the mentor is a better, more capable person and will always be better and more capable. Constant negative comparison with a mentor destroys the atmosphere of respectful equality that should exist in the workplace. It can also destroy self-esteem.

So it's important to choose a mentor wisely, and to understand that mentor relationships change as people grow. If you find yourself in a mentor relationship that has soured, the best approach is usually to sit down with that person and discuss the situation openly.

In its best form, the mentor/protégé relationship is good for the people involved and for the company. The mentor has the satisfaction of passing along his or her wisdom and experience. The protégé receives valuable training and guidance. The company benefits from having two dedicated employees who are helping each other work more productively.

But it's important to realize that, as in all human relations, there is a potential negative result. The best way to avoid a negative result is to be careful and honest, and to treat a mentor as a professional resource without giving up personal autonomy and responsibility.

◆ Recognition of a Career Dead End Is a Key to Personal Growth

If you were driving down a road that suddenly came to a dead end, you would no doubt turn your car around and find some alternative route to reach your destination. Yet when people drive into dead ends in their careers, they often keep right on going, slamming themselves into a wall of frustration and unhappiness and emerging battered, bruised and jobless.

Of course, when you're driving a car, a dead-end street is obvious and is probably marked with signs long before you get to the dead end. The dead ends you encounter as you navigate through a career are much more difficult to recognize, but the signs are there if you know what to look for.

First, a definition is in order. As I see it, a dead-end job (or career for that matter) is one in which an individual ceases to personally grow.

Although personal growth is something that can be defined only by the individual, it certainly is not defined simply as more money and a bigger title. It is easy to acquire those things and still be at a dead end. Your personal growth is more likely measured by how much your job enhances your personal life and sense of well-being.

A lack of growth also is likely to be manifested in physical, intellectual and emotional symptoms which become the danger signs of a career dead end. You might start having recurring headaches, indigestion or insomnia. You might constantly procrastinate or become overly industrious. More commonly, you might start having problems at home.

If you suspect you are at a dead end, the first thing to do is take a long, hard look at whether your relationships with your spouse, family, friends and loved ones are just as comfortable as ever. If not, there may be career-related issues you are not dealing with and frustrations being vented off the job. It has been estimated that 80 to 90 percent of all personal problems are caused by career problems that people simply don't want to acknowledge.

Next, ask yourself if you still like and respect your boss. A change in your relationship with your boss is a clear sign of trouble, as is a change in your relationships with your subordinates and co-workers. These changes can be extremely subtle, but are nonetheless felt by everyone. What's more, they often are ignored and, as a result, the tensions they create just grow worse.

All of this relates to a dead end in which you become burned out, even though your employer might be perfectly happy with the job you are doing.

But there is another kind of dead end: You're happy with your job, but suddenly find yourself unemployed. Firings in these circumstances are absolutely devastating to the individual. The fact is, however, most of them are foreseeable.

The key in this situation is the relationship with your boss. In order to be happy with a job, everyone must have accountability, responsibility and authority. Accountability cannot be delegated by a superior, but responsibility and authority can.

When authority is withdrawn, it should be a red flag that the boss has lost confidence and trouble is on the way. Unfortunately, it usually happens slowly and subtly, so it takes a politically astute mind to recognize what's going on.

One of the more overt signs of trouble occurs when your boss becomes inaccessible to you. If he or she becomes too busy to see you at important times, you should rightfully wonder how important your work is in the boss's eyes.

Learn too, to be aware of the political atmosphere at work. People often are unwilling to believe that one of their co-workers might have it in for them and let the situation build itself into a dead end.

I remember a client who was responsible for major accomplishments within his company, but who, in the course of his achievements, roused the ire of a vice president who feared competition for his job. This VP began dropping subtle hints to others about my client's ineptness and sought out ways to turn in bad reports about the man. A negative atmosphere soon developed, and eventually, this man lost his job — an eventuality he should have seen coming.

I also have seen instances of "reverse dead ends" — that is, a case in which someone feels trapped or unhappy on the job because of personal problems.

There is no question that people going through a divorce or other major life trauma can bring their problems to work.

Usually though, work allows a person to make a daily escape from the problems at home. Even when things go wrong on the personal side, most people continue to do reasonably well on the job. Besides, most companies are sensitive enough to this sort of thing to recognize it and to be somewhat patient about it. Reverse dead ends are rare.

Dead ends are not easy to spot. Sometimes good old gut feeling is the best way to know when you have hit one. Just remember to keep your eyes and ears open at all times, and be ready to take charge if you have to.

♦ How to Recover from a Career Mistake

All of us make mistakes in our careers. (The monumental ones — spending half our lives in the wrong field — require the most courageous and forthright action; see, for example, Chapter Two, *Controlling Your Own Career Moves.*) Other mistakes, such as sending a customer the wrong spec sheet or being late for a meeting, have little or no effect on our careers. Still others, like the mistake made by a man who in a fit of anger voted himself out of his own company, have long-lasting consequences.

All of us make mistakes in our careers.

This man had controlling interest in a company which he had founded and built into a large, profitable firm. However, he made a series of errors which led to his bigger mistake. First, he gradually sold his stock until he owned only 35 percent of the company. Second, he allowed some of the shares to slip into the hands of a few stockholders who were continually trying to vote him out of the company. He eventually became so tired of the constant bickering that he voted his shares with those who were trying to get rid of him. He was out of a job.

Of course, once his anger passed, he was devastated. He had no income, no job and no way to get the money he'd invested in his company. The only way he could continue to support his family was to accept his daughter's gift of a trust fund that had been established for her. The more he thought about the situation, the more despondent he became, even to the point of seriously considering suicide.

Recovering from a career mistake requires several steps:

First, admit the mistake — openly and honestly. We all prefer to find reasons why someone else was responsible for our mistakes. It is a fact that others usually contribute to our mistakes. In some cases they may be more than 50 percent responsible. But before we can recover from a mistake, we must accept our own responsibility. We alone determine our own behavior.

Second, analyze the damage. Usually the seriousness of a mistake is directly related to the boss's perception of how much it has cost him or her and the company. Not just in money, but in tarnished reputation, internal strife, reduced standing in the community. If the mistake is restricted to hurting the boss's pride, communicating a forthright repentant attitude will oftentimes bring about full repair. In the prior instance, however, it may well require both the repentant attitude as well as taking steps — perhaps requested of and suggested by the boss — designed to repair the damage. But if a mistake resulted in a substantial loss in these areas, it may be difficult to fix, and it may mean finding a new job.

Third, learn from the mistake. Or, to put it another way, analyze the internal damage to yourself. We all like to say that we learn from our mistakes, but it frequently is passed off in simple terms of, "I made a mistake, I know it, now I'm tougher." The entire process of admitting a mistake includes analyzing how it happened and how to keep it from happening again, but more importantly, acknowledging the extent of damage to our pride, the diminished self-confidence, the extent of embarrassment in dealing with those who were affected by the mistake. One of the most common problems we see in our consulting business is the person who is unable to admit any such personal negative effect and who therefore doesn't deal with it. In effect this "closes over" an open wound which, unhealed, "festers" in the subconscious. Give it some air. Look at it. Admit it. Deal with it.

Fourth, avoid dwelling on the mistake. This seems a contradiction to the previous point, but it is not. Learning from a mistake shouldn't mean allowing it to damage your self-esteem. Once you have squarely and honestly acknowledged a mistake, have recognized your honest feelings about it, and have gone beyond the initial defensive posture, you have to avoid replaying the mistake over and over. The way to do this is to take time to remember all the times you didn't make that mistake. If we all sat down and listed the times we did something poorly and then listed the times we did something quite well, the success list would be much longer than the mistake list.

Fifth, forgive yourself. It is sad to see people who berate themselves endlessly for their failures. This self-forgiveness will occur in the process of doing what is suggested in the third and fourth points.

Sixth, develop a plan of action and stick to it. If the mistake means finding a new job, what kind of a job will it be and what is the best way to go about finding it? If the mistake means repairing some bruised relationships, spend time talking to the people the mistake affected. Admit the mistake, apologize for any trouble it caused them, and ask for their help in avoiding the mistake in the future. Ask what steps you can take in repairing the damage.

Let me return to the man I mentioned earlier. Because of the stark honesty with which he faced his internal hurt and the damage to his pride, and because he was then able to set it aside and objectively reassess years of high level success, he regained his composure and had an excellent position *within a month.*

The entire process of learning from a mistake includes analyzing how it happened and how to keep it from happening again; but more importantly, acknowledging the extent of damage to pride and self-confidence.

If you are going to make mistakes — and we all do — make energetic, active mistakes. People who make mistakes because they are vigorously plunging into their assigned challenges are easier to forgive (and can more easily forgive themselves) than people who make mistakes from lack of initiative or lack of focus. We've all heard many, many times that mistakes are inevitable, that they are part of learning and growing. But not until we really believe this will we be able to be effective managers and employees.

"... For the first time in my career, I know that I am in control. I no longer will have to sit on one job thinking about how great it would be somewhere else. Now I know about the 'somewhere elses.' Even if a new idea surfaces, I now know how to research it for results ..."

K. G., *Client*

CHAPTER EIGHT

Coping With Internal Forces

I have met the enemy and he is me.
—Anon.

KnowThyself.
— Socrates

♦ Career Problems and Personal Life

Eighty to ninety percent of all personal problems are caused by career problems. Counselors experienced in both personal and career counseling tend to agree with this statement. Most of our waking hours (and some of our sleeping hours) are taken up with job or career — time spent involved in our work, or thinking about it.

It's common for people to adhere to the notion that their careers and personal lives are completely separate; that one has nothing to do with the other. I seriously doubt that this is possible. The two simply cannot be separated.

We all have tremendous ego identification with our careers. The way we use our talents defines the way we are judged by society and how we are seen by our peers. When we have problems with our careers it *must* affect our egos. And that invariably leads to personal problems.

Unfortunately, because of this ego identification, people will initially deny that there is any problem at work. After all, it's socially unacceptable to hate a job that defines one's self. It somehow seems easier to blame a marriage for personal problems than it is to blame a job.

Spouses need to be particularly attentive to the danger signs of career problems. Men in particular tend to become silent and withdrawn. Their career problems might make them feel weak and vulnerable — socially unacceptable feelings for a man to have — so they will assume a posture of being unfeeling and unaffected. And I'm sure I needn't explain where lack of communication leads a marriage.

Less common, though frequently seen, is the man who becomes hyperactive, burying himself in extracurricular activities and pushing himself to the brink of exhaustion. His purpose in so doing, of course, is to avoid serious communication on career-related issues.

**The majority of personal problems,
including marital problems,
are caused by career and job problems.**

Conversely, women seem more likely to want to talk about what's going on and will seek out someone on whom to vent their rage and hostilities. In a good relationship, a man can encourage his wife to unload on him. But many men, I have found, can't do this.

Common to both men and women are sleep disorders. An inability to fall asleep, trouble waking up, and waking up before the alarm goes off can all be signs of career-related stress.

Perhaps I should stop here and say that there are indeed cases — a minority I believe — in which personal problems destroy careers. It's not unusual to see people who enjoy and do well in their jobs develop drug or alcohol problems that ruin their careers.

But it's also not unusual to see people with serious personal problems use their work as an escape. One man I worked with many years ago was simultaneously dealing with a divorce and a suicide in his family, yet he was able to go to work every day and carry it off beautifully. Work for him was a respite from the troubles he faced at home.

I suppose there are as many different reactions to personal problems as there are people, but the bottom line is this: Before we look to our marriages and our families as the causes of our problems, we must look to ourselves and our careers.

If someone we know is withdrawn or lashing out, we must presume that they are hurting very badly inside, and rather than withdrawing or lashing back ourselves, we owe it to them to raise serious questions about their jobs and careers. Not just once but many, many times.

The pressures that cause career problems can be monumental. But they are not eased by kicking the dog or screaming at a spouse. Understanding what's really going on is an important first step toward doing something about it.

◆ Moving Out of Comfort Zones

How comfortable are you with your job and career?

Most of you reading this probably make a decent living and would answer that question, "Very comfortable."

The fact is, many people define comfort by the amount of money they make. If they make a "comfortable living," they profess to be comfortable with their jobs.

Money, the regular paycheck, is perhaps the most pervasive of the many "comfort zones" into which people settle and from which they find it difficult to move, no matter how great the need to move may be. It's a major reason why studies have found 80 to 90 percent of us are unhappy with our jobs.

I suppose a historian might see a very natural evolution of this attitude in America. This country was built on a pioneer spirit that pushed people to risk everything they had and brave incredible hardships in order to explore new frontiers. After a while, though, there were no other frontiers to conquer, and the pioneer spirit, with its survival instinct and rugged individualism, gave way to a settlement mentality. The pioneers ceased to be pioneers and instead became settlers.

Life may have been hard for the early settlers, but they developed the ethic that as long as their needs were taken care of, they had nothing to complain about. This is the same kind of ethic that has stayed with us to this day.

We settle for those job and career comfort zones that may be less than what we truly want because "they pay well," or "it's a nice place to work," or "I couldn't make this much money doing something else."

We settle into the comfort zone of doing what we've been educated to do because "I paid a lot of money to get that degree and to not use it would be throwing that money away." This, of course, is ridiculous. Our educational experiences help mold us into the people we are, regardless of what field we're in.

We settle into the comfort zones created by family pressure, particularly in the case of the children of professionals who feel that they must also be professionals, even if they are better suited to other options.

How can you define your own comfort zones? As with most career issues, it's a matter of stark self-honesty. When you merely settle for a comfort zone, you will have misgivings along certain lines — an awareness that there are greater challenges that could be met in your career.

Comfort zones also create routines, boredom and lack of energy in both personal and professional life. There may even be a subtle loss of self-esteem.

A person caught up in a comfort zone is someone who is simply not growing, as comfort zones do not permit growth. And the comfort of taking home the paycheck and getting those pats on the head from the boss while having our personal growth stifled may create additional internal conflicts.

Meanwhile, as technology expands and changes, we may find ourselves even more anxious to find comfort zones, as the pressure to keep up with the rapidly changing workplace may simply be too great.

Whatever state of mind we've grown into, comfort zones are something each individual needs to rethink. What's needed now is a new kind of pioneer spirit that allows, even pushes, an individual to plunge forward into new fields of endeavor — a new adventurism that allows us to use our talents more effectively.

One of the most eye-opening experiences of my life came many years ago during a four-day cruise up the Amazon River. Many of the people we saw and visited along the shore during that trip wore nothing but loincloths and carried what were, at best, primitive tools. Most Americans would consider them a backward civilization.

But looking at them and reflecting on the pain I often hear from my own clients, I knew that in a certain sense they were far more advanced than we. There was a calm about them, a sense of peace. They were simply satisfied with their lives and confident in their ability to meet their daily challenges. They had a deeply ingrained and unchanged value system, and they had no need to seek and settle for comfort zones. Neither do you.

◆ Mental Blocks to Freedom of Choice

Without objective awareness of our emotions and motivations, we can never enjoy the freedom of choice that lets us get what we really want from life.

> **The freedom to choose,**
> **which will get us**
> **what we really want**
> **in career and life,**
> **requires a clear and objective awareness**
> **of our own emotions and motivations.**

Unfortunately, we set up many mental blocks for ourselves that keep us from achieving this kind of self-knowledge. Perhaps by understanding some of these obstacles, we can more easily overcome them.

First and foremost is **fear.** It may be unconscious, but it is fear nonetheless.

We fear that if we fail at what we really want to do, it will hurt considerably more than sticking with something we do not really like. We fear that if we look too deeply within ourselves we will not like what we see. We fear unpleasant memories that we work hard to suppress. So we find our comfort zones and milk them for all they're worth.

Second is **self-image,** implanted in childhood. Erroneous perceptions of self, developed as children, are carried with us well into adulthood and prevent us from realizing our full potential.

Third is our general **inability to communicate,** especially with ourselves. Lack of self-communication prevents us from freely identifying our own values. Instead, we unquestioningly adopt the values of our parents, our schools, our peers, etc. We then become so steeped in the thinking and vocabulary of the field we're in that we often find it impossible to communicate with those outside the field. Ultimately, however, career success comes down to a matter of communication.

Lastly is **denial.** For the most part, we find it easier to deny that we have feelings which might be considered socially unacceptable (i.e. hatred of one's job) than to confront and deal with those feelings head on.

A standout in this regard is a man who, for two years, had systematically made all of the mistakes necessary to get himself fired, but he could never admit to himself that he was doing this since such actions run so strongly against the societal grain. It's far easier to subconsciously create external forces and then blame them for our misfortune.

Another case history from many years ago summarizes much of what I'm talking about here. My client in this instance had been a Royal Air Force colonel who was an expert in survival techniques. Upon leaving the service, he tried to make his way by teaching such techniques, but found virtually no market for it.

Eventually, he took a job selling solar heating equipment, rationalizing that converting people to alternative energy was a survival issue. It was a living (although not much of one), but certainly not what he really wanted.

Here's what was going on: During World War II, he had been a field sergeant in Europe. While talking to two other sergeants on the fringe of a battlefield, the lead sergeant took a direct hit from an enemy shell and was instantly reduced to a bloody mass. The other sergeant, who was second in command, went berserk, leaving my client in charge. From that time forward, this man had been questioning the survivor mentality, perhaps feeling guilty about having come through the incident unscathed while the other two men had not.

Once he was able to face this head-on, he was able to see that what he really wanted was to study the survivor mentality, research it and write about it. Eventually, he received a fellowship from a major university to do exactly that.

This, of course, is an extreme case, but it does illustrate the point. We all put up mental blocks that hamper our career decisions. Without understanding these mental blocks, we can never truly have that freedom.

Emotions are strange things. When we honestly acknowledge their presence, we control them. If we try to ignore them, they control us. However, if we acknowledge the presence of an emotion and see a reason for overcoming it, chances are that we will. It is a difficult task, but it is well worth the reward: Freedom of choice.

♦ **The Cop-Out Syndrome**

Our failure to deal honestly with problems at work which cause us pain frequently leads us to a cop-out.

Have you ever said any of the following things with regard to your job?

"I have no right to complain. After all, I'm doing better than most people."

"There's nothing wrong. I just need a vacation."

"I couldn't do this well anywhere else."

"I love my work. The problem is my boss/spouse/kids/parents — but that'll change."

All of these commonly heard laments — and many others like them — are spoken by people who have fallen victim to what I call the "career cop-out syndrome."

Put simply, we put off things that may be distasteful or that lead to rejection. We find excuses not to take action. Rather than take charge of our careers, we cop-out.

I'm reminded of a young man I once saw in the lobby of a downtown office building in Chicago. He dejectedly leaned against the wall, staring at his shoes, cradling his attaché case. Whenever some one walked by, he would straighten up and walk about the lobby as if he were ready to conquer the world. Then, once again out of anyone's sight, he would again slump against the wall.

This man was waiting to make a sales call, but just couldn't bring himself to do it. "Yes," he could say in the presence of others, "I'm a dynamic person and a crackerjack salesman."

Inside, however, he was frightened, reluctant and probably not very happy. Rather than admit it, though, he put on his suit and tie and presented an image that wasn't true.

There are times, of course, when all of us genuinely do need a vacation. But I truly believe that in nine out of ten cases, rather than forcing ourselves to be honest about what we really want, we just take some form of cop-out.

Highly competent people are especially susceptible to an ego identification with their jobs, leading to a less-than-accurate awareness of their true feelings about their work.

How can you recognize the cop-out syndrome in yourself? With great difficulty, apparently. Most people don't recognize it until they're hit between the eyes with a 2 x 4 (i.e., fired). I suppose if you find yourself constantly repeating some of the lines I used at the outset, that's a sure sign. Or, if you keep telling yourself you're happy but you suffer from physical or emotional symptoms such as ulcers, insomnia, headaches, an inability to relax at work and constant brooding at home about things going on in the office, you might be suffering from the cop-out syndrome.

Highly competent people, I have found, are especially susceptible to this problem. As I've said before, there is intense ego identification with our jobs. What's more, when we're good at something, we're expected to like it no matter what. The more experience we amass, the stronger the societal pressure to stick with it. Besides, disliking one's job is simply not a socially acceptable emotion.

On the other hand, people can be painfully aware of what's going on and find themselves unable to act on their feelings because they're afraid they can't do anything to change their predicament. They fall into what I call the "just-a" syndrome. You've heard it a thousand times, I'm sure. "I'm just a teacher." "I'm just a lawyer." "I'm just a housewife."

This is a particularly vicious cop-out in that people restrict their vision as to what they *could be*, settling instead for what they see as their "lot in life." They allow themselves to be dominated by their situation, rather than controlling it.

"It's a great company. Why would I want to leave? Besides, I'm just about due for a raise and/or promotion."

This is yet another cop-out. And no matter how bad situations might get, people cop-out by telling themselves they are happy. They tell themselves that their field — and especially their company — is *the* best. But let's face it, though I believe in loyalty to one's company (and vice versa), in the final analysis we work only for ourselves.

Happiness is an elusive and intangible state of mind. But given the incredible choices open to all of us regarding career, there's simply no reason to proclaim happiness to others, then suffer in silence. Things can *always* be better. You *can* be perfectly happy in your job and career, or at least strive toward that as a goal.

And next time you hear yourself say, "The money's good, and it's a nice place to work," ask yourself if you really mean that or if you're just copping out. Force yourself to be honest.

♦ Scapegoating

In ancient times, the Jewish people had a religious ritual in which a high priest would transfer the sins of a congregation to the head of a goat which would then be sacrificed or allowed to escape into the wilderness. In this way, they believed, they were absolved of their sins and of the blame for their sins.

From this practice comes the modern word "scapegoat," which Webster's Dictionary defines as, "A person or thing bearing blame for others."

If I may use the word as a verb, "scapegoating" is the practice of blaming others for our failures. In career terms, there is far too much scapegoating going on in the world today.

Let's face it, the most successful people are those who have the ability to stand outside themselves and objectively assess how good they are at one thing or how they are lacking in another. Unfortunately, there are not as many truly successful people as there could be.

Instead, people find scapegoats to blame for their failings. It is, after all, much easier to blame a bad boss or inept employees for problems. It's probably just human nature to do so. But scapegoating is unproductive. Worse, it's a hindrance to a successful career.

The only productive stance to take is to openly acknowledge that there are problems and to assume that the fault lies with all concerned, including yourself. Realize next that what you can do to change other people is very limited. On the other hand, you have full control over your own actions.

Whether or not you have the degree of self-honesty that's needed to acknowledge your failings and take action is another matter altogether. When people get into problem situations in their careers, they frequently get into a paranoid state of mind from which it is very difficult to get out. The aura of suspicion that hovers over the situation makes honest communication —with yourself as well as with others — virtually impossible. In the process of blaming everyone around them, people fail to see a much greater truth — that they would probably be better off working somewhere else or doing something else. As a result, people do not act on their problems until the problems have gotten out of hand. Most firings or resignations occur at least six months after they should have.

Confidence and self-honesty go hand in hand.

In fact, it's one of the saddest things I see in my career consulting practice: The person who blames all kinds of external forces for his or her problems rather than looking inward.

Why do people find scapegoats? Perhaps, as I said earlier, it's human nature. More likely, it's lack of self-honesty and lack of confidence. And as much as anything, employers hire *confidence*.

Confidence and self-honesty go hand in hand. After all, if a person is good and knows it, he or she is merely stating a fact and can't be held at fault for stating it. What's more, confident, honest people waste little time with scapegoating. They're too successful for that. If you are a manager, you have no doubt interviewed this kind of person, and more often than not, you have actually perceived such a person as being rather humble.

Conversely, you've probably interviewed people who let you know how good they are, but also spent a good deal of time scapegoating — blaming everything and everyone but themselves for the problems they had with previous employers or co-workers. You probably perceived these people simply as braggarts.

People who are honest and confident need no scapegoats. Those with internal image problems and lack of confidence will always find them somewhere.

Here's a case in point: Many years ago, a man came to us with a severe confidence problem. We encourage people to move strongly in making contacts and to go out and present themselves, something this man, because he lacked confidence, did not want to do. Naturally he had great difficulty finding a new job using the methods we teach, because he didn't use them. And lo and behold, we became his scapegoat. He couldn't find work, he claimed, because the methods we had given him didn't work.

He clung zealously to this belief for a long time — two or three years as I recall — and our relationship with him was often acrimonious at best.

Finally, as if in a single revelatory burst, he realized that he was blaming something other than himself for the fear he felt and that as long as he continued to do so, his career would go nowhere.

With his scapegoat cast aside, his confidence level soared. He found a new — and much better — job in short order.

Think about this the next time you find yourself unhappy in your career and you blame others for your unhappiness. Take that energy you waste in scapegoating and devote it to learning something you don't know about yourself.

It could be your pathway to career happiness.

◆ The Illusory Self

"Know Thyself" is one of humankind's oldest admonitions, perhaps because so few of us ever do know ourselves. However, it may be the most important advice given to anyone considering a major career move.

In order to be happy and successful in your career, it is

imperative that you be honest with yourself, see through what can be called your "illusory self," and get at your real self.

Defined simply, the illusory self is the person you perceive yourself to be or the person you wish you were, rather than the person you really are. The illusory self tends to be particularly overpowering in highly competent people who mold themselves to fit their functions and who make their career moves by tailoring themselves to what they think is available rather than to what they really want.

I suppose it's natural to be somewhat afraid of what we might find if we look deep within ourselves: Anxiety, stress, dissatisfaction, anger. These are feelings that we're taught from childhood that should be hidden or suppressed, not freely expressed when it comes to career. As a result, we put a great deal of energy into our facades without ever examining what's beneath them. The key is to stop trying to be what you think you have to be to keep your job, and instead, be yourself in a job that's suited to you.

**Defined simply, the illusory self is the person
you perceive yourself to be
or the person you wish you were,
rather than the person you really are.**

Here's an exercise you might try with a spouse or close friend who will help you see past your illusory self. This exercise is designed to stimulate conversation, not provide easy answers, since it is only by talking and sharing our feelings with others that we can truly communicate.

For each of the following five items, rate yourself on a scale of one to six, with one being exceptional and six being poor. Have a close friend or spouse rate you with the same scale, then discuss — and I mean really discuss — your conclusions. (Bear in mind that others may rate you lower than you rate yourself, since people who are close to you have seen you at your worst and are likely to remember it more than you do.)

1. Decisiveness. Chooses among available courses of actions without extensive periods of perplexity, indecision, hesitation, vacillation. Does not procrastinate.

2. Objectivity. Accurately identifies and predicts the behavior of others without distortion and without intermingling his own subjective urgencies.

3. Strength of will. In spite of consequent difficulties, persists in completing what he has resolved to do. Starts anew after failure without undue self-incrimination.

4. Self control. Is capable, as necessary, of restraining or modifying impulses, emotions or feelings that are unacceptable. On the other hand, is capable of expressing basically enjoyable or satisfying tendencies without guilt, anxiety or conflict.

5. Organizing ability. Lives an ordered life. Avoids haphazard action. Schedules and organizes, makes plans and follows them.

Now, I'm not going to draw any conclusions for you based on what your answers might look like. These are intended to be thought and discussion starters that will help you be honest about yourself. But here's some more food for thought:

If you rated yourself a point or more lower on decisiveness than your friend did, it could indicate a poor self-image. The roots of poor self-image are often found in career issues, but can also be found in things beyond the scope of career counseling.

It's natural for friends and spouses to rate you low on objectivity since they consistently see you at your least objective. Again, this is merely meant to be a discussion starter.

People who are hurting or suffering from feelings of anxiety or self-incrimination often rate themselves low on strength of will. A little more soul-searching to determine why is in order.

A high rating for self-control is common since, as I said earlier, we're taught to suppress negative feelings even in childhood.

A low rating from friends might not necessarily be significant, since they see us at our most uninhibited.

A high rating for organizing ability might be taken as a negative by some, as many in our society place a premium on spontaneity. I believe, however, that most employers consider it to be a positive.

The list I provided in this exercise can be expanded. Indeed, you may want to come up with your own list of qualities and work through it with a friend or spouse.

If there's anything you can do to help yourself see through your illusory self, do it. Living behind the facade of your illusory self will never bring you true success.

♦ Emotional Gyrations in Career Moves

All the forces and factors mentioned above can cause a major negative impact on us at the simple thought of a career change.

So if you're thinking about making a career move, be aware that you're about to step aboard an emotional roller coaster that will provide you with excitement, apprehension and a greater sense of personal pride. No matter how much individuals and their career moves might differ, there are some predictable emotional upheavals.

Unfortunately, most people either tend to deny what's happening to them or they get swept away in an unexpected flood of emotions. By clearly facing what's going on, it's possible either to use those emotions in a positive way or move forcefully to counteract them. In either case, a career move becomes easier to deal with, both for you and those around you.

A common first reaction is intense stress brought on by the denial of the need to make a change. When I start working with new clients, I ask them how long ago they first realized that a career move was in order. The usual reply is three or four months.

Later, as they deal with it more objectively, they almost always acknowledge that they should have realized it three or four (in one case, twenty-some) years earlier.

We tend to deny that we have career problems for three basic reasons:

1.) Facing them could upset our lives too much; 2.) it's easier to blame other things and people for the stress we have; and 3.) our egos drive us to be successful at whatever we're doing, no matter how much we dislike it. Admitting that a job is the cause of stress looks too much like failure.

Gradually, however, at least an awareness develops that the job is indeed the cause of the stress and eventually we come to a stark realization. This leads in most cases to the second reaction: A strong level of fear.

"Will I be able to cope with what I have to do?" is the question everyone grapples with.

The fear can sometimes be debilitating. Most people, however, come to grips with it and experience the third emotion: The beginning of a sense of excitement.

I liken this to the feeling you would have if leaving your hometown for the first time to go to a foreign country where you do not speak the language. You know you will experience some difficulties, but you know that it will be exhilarating and you know you will come through the experience alive. And, of course, everyone comes through their career moves alive and better off for them.

This sense of excitement later settles into a feeling of confidence and peace as people start reassessing their situation and deciding what they would really like to do. People stop using others as scapegoats for their problems, start making objective decisions about their careers, and consequently, feel a greater sense of control.

No matter how much you might feel you control the situation, though, the fear returns. First comes a fear of the decisions you have made. Was it really the right one? Are you making a wrong turn?

Then comes a fear of rejection.

Although positive responses to your marketing efforts can be a great motivator, many people are paralyzed by this fear and take a good deal of time to begin their contacts. Excuses become the order of the day.

**Examine any company
and you will probably find
a greater number of divorced people
than those who have quit a job
or made a career change.**

An ex-CEO I worked with years ago kept putting off his job search so he could organize his notes. He must have had the world's best-organized notes, since it took him nearly six months to do it. Another former client decided to use his period of unemployment to paint his house, spending a week on (hiding in) each room.

These men were immobilized by fear, plain and simple. Though they had ascended to the highest levels of their industries, they were rendered helpless by their own fear. Both eventually solved their problem: They honestly acknowledged their fear and overcame it.

Finally, of course, is the exhilaration of finding a new job, or making the sought-after career change.

Many parts of our lives other than career follow the same pattern described here. But for some reason, things are different when it comes to career. Examine any company and you will probably find a much larger number of people who are divorced than have ever quit a job or made a career change.

We seem to find it easy — even socially acceptable — to redesign our personal situations, but not our career situations. It's probably due to the intense ego identification we have with our jobs. The more intense such identification is, the more intense the emotions are when it comes time for a change.

Change is inevitable. Awareness of what to expect can only make the process easier.

♦ Surviving a Career Crash

A career might rightly be thought of as a highway down which each of us drives, weaving our way in and out of traffic and moving ever closer to our ultimate destination: Success.

But the road isn't always smooth. It can be fraught with hazards, reckless drivers, sharp curves and long uphill grades. And no matter how carefully you drive, there's a good chance that at some point, you'll crash.

Career crashes are almost always survivable. In fact, if handled properly, most people come out of them stronger than ever and driving down their career highway faster than they did prior to the crash. That's not to say it isn't a painful experience or that the wounds heal quickly. They do heal, however.

A career crash usually occurs when you are fired or, if you own your own business, your business fails. Few things in life are more stressful or more devastating.

Now, this should be differentiated from hitting a dead end. Most people who hit dead ends sooner or later realize what has happened and retain a sense of control. That sense of control is all-important in making career moves. People who go through career crashes experience an abject loss of control and with it feelings of shame, humiliation, failure and anger.

Many of the people I work with have just been through a career crash. In fact, I suppose a major reason career consultants exist is to help people through those times.

Unfortunately, most try to paint a happy face on the situation and pretend the crash didn't really happen. Usually we will say it no longer bothers us and we move ahead with finding a new job immediately. Inevitably, though, we are all hampered by the feelings of shame and failure.

**Surviving a career crash
takes toughness, humility and honesty.
The urge to hide must be fought tooth and nail,
as must the urge to go back
and try to reclaim the wreckage.**

The way to overcome it, of course, is to face those feelings squarely, with a large dose of humility. Be rudely honest with yourself. Realize that career crashes happen to everybody and you just have to start again.

Systematically examine all of your options. Apply for any unemployment benefits that might be due you, no matter how distasteful this process might seem to be. Write down all of your investments and assets on a piece of paper. Most people, upon doing this, find that their financial situation isn't as bad as they first thought it was, and that relieves a great deal of stress. Avoid blaming scapegoats or circumstances beyond your control. Look forward, not backward.

Then be ready to shed some honest tears. I often tell spouses that if they can help their mate cry about the situation, he or she has really faced the problem. This is easier said than done for men who, for the most part, consider crying unacceptable behavior. It does, however, relieve a tremendous emotional burden.

Next, avoid the urge to hide. There is no shame in a career crash, nor is there any shame in seeking help, whether from a friend, a spouse or a professional.

I once briefly worked with a man who had been fired and given the option of coming to me as part of his outplacement package. His pride would not let him acknowledge that he needed help. Instead, he decided he deserved six months off and spent his time doing literally nothing. When he finally did come in to see me, he was destitute and his marriage was in ruins. I saw him for only a couple of sessions before he decided once again that he did not need help. Although I did not hear from him again, I suspect that he did not "survive" his crash.

In a contrasting case, I worked with a 62-year-old man who had been forced into early retirement. Given his vivacity, it was no different than being fired. This man, a widower, dealt with his pain not by squarely facing his career crash, but by marrying his deceased best friend's wife. Needless to say, this marriage of convenience did nothing to heal the wounds from his crash, nor did it restore the vigor he'd lost when he lost his job.

He eventually realized that he had made a mistake, and after some heart-rending self-examination faced his feelings of failure head-on. He again became spry and lively, and when I last heard from him he was the president of a company for the first time in his life.

Surviving a career crash takes toughness, humility and honesty. The urge to hide must be fought tooth and nail, as must the urge to go back and try to reclaim the wreckage. It can be an uphill battle, but it is a fight that almost everyone wins.

◆ Overcome Denial to Be Free in Career

Denial is a common human defense mechanism. It basically means that a person is not acknowledging what is true about self or a situation, and is trying to live as though it were different than it really is. Denial may be more prevalent in career activities and decisions than most other kinds of human endeavor.

Denial related to oneself falls into three different categories: Denial of our own abilities; denial of our weaknesses and failures; and denial of the circumstances in which we live and act. Denial traps a person. The solution is to be found in living by the truism, "The truth will set you free." It is common for us as career consultants to work with clients who fail to acknowledge their own abilities. Individuals often spend years feeling that they could do more than they have, and consequently feel vaguely but intensely dissatisfied. They feel they have unused talents, but have never gathered the courage or taken the time to identify those talents.

Some clients with no previous managerial experience become managers after they reflect and examine themselves in depth. Others are secretaries who do not consider themselves able to do anything beyond clerical work, but become highly productive sales people. Still others who were never top managers become company presidents for the first time. One of our classic cases, mentioned earlier, is the man who became a company president for the first time in his life at the age of 63.

The feeling by individuals that they are not using their talents or that they are not being challenged causes erosion of self-confidence. It is a gradual occurrence and is usually ignored. When we suggest to our clients there is evidence that they can aspire to much greater heights, we are frequently told that family and friends have been repeating the same thing for years — but the client has chosen not to believe them.

In such cases, we must support our clients in those activities which will help them re-develop (or develop for the first time) an objective, positive self-image. A series of advisors stretching back into childhood (teachers, parents, spouses) suggesting that one could do more, is a good sign that a person could quite literally do so.

It is frustrating and a matter of self-betrayal for a person to suspect that he or she has great talent and not take positive steps to identify it and develop it. This failure to act tears down personal confidence and, in a psychological snowballing effect, makes it ever more difficult for a person to escape the entrapment.

The second area of denial has to do with weaknesses. When people don't admit their weaknesses, they can't actively try to shore them up. While it may be difficult to admit our abilities, it is even harder to admit to weaknesses because our all-too-human egos get in the way.

One weakness people don't want to face is a low self-image or lack of self-confidence. It can be quite embarrassing for us to admit that we do not give ourselves credit for capabilities we objectively possess.

Here is an (unusual) example of how this can work against a person:

A man we worked with years ago had made his own fortune in a relatively short period of time. When his wife of 25 to 30 years died, he became morose, fell into depression, lost his entire fortune and ended up homeless. He lived on the street for a few years until he started slowly to heal. While he felt better after he got a job and a place to live, he still had not repaired emotionally. Whenever we addressed the fact that he had not regained his confidence, he angrily denied the idea. It required intense effort to help him admit that the problem remained. Finally, after extensive reflection, he honestly acknowledged his low self-esteem and began a rapid recovery.

It can be quite embarrassing for us to admit that we do not give ourselves credit for capabilities we possess.

It is the weaknesses we are unwilling to face which ultimately control us and hold us back. Unacknowledged, they prevent us from studying how to strengthen or compensate for them. We can find out about our weaknesses in two ways: Listen carefully to our opponents' views of us; or ask (pay) someone to be frank with us.

The third subject of denial is our current circumstances. This is what puts so many square pegs in round holes in our society and causes so many people to simply "put up with" distasteful jobs. We don't want to admit we made a mistake, that we are in the wrong field, that parental insistence that we become lawyers (dentists, doctors, teachers) might have been wrong. We find it hard to admit that we are hurting. One client's wife pointed out to him that for ten years, he had not liked what he was doing. He was at first astonished and maintained that it was only a year or two. She insisted that it was ten years, and he finally acknowledged that she was right.

We have heard people express deep affection for the companies in which they have spent 15 to 20 or more years, but ultimately realize they detested them all that time. We have known others who repeatedly made mistakes and were fired after a series of warnings. After dealing with their anger, they realized that they actually brought it on themselves. Some people deny the family circumstances they grew up in. They don't want to remember the abuses that were perpetrated on them by parents, siblings and teachers.

All of these forces remain buried in the subconscious. They persist as subtle but enormous weaknesses.

It is hard to admit that our career situations are less than perfect; our fears and various social pressures force us to find contentment in what we have — or at least put up with it. The majority of us conclude that since we cannot decide what else to do we will simply continue to do what we have been doing. Or we retain superficial help (including preference tests, a few college courses, a workshop) which will confirm the decision to make no real changes.

Denial is one of the most difficult problems that people face in life. If you are in a denial mode, you will never take care of the problem. The keynote is clear, honest awareness of what we are, what we're good at, what we're not good at. The truth, clearly perceived in this fashion, will make any of us free in our career choices and actions.

**It requires a special effort
to unlock ourselves from all the forces which affect us,
boldly choose what we want to do,
and then achieve a predetermined goal
within the marketplace.**

"... I was unhappy with my business career. I wanted to go into something entirely different in order to get out of the rut I was in. Through your intensive program I was able to explore thousands of possibilities. I learned to look at my business and my career from a different perspective. I no longer felt trapped ... I used my imagination and thought about what I would most like to do if I could do anything in the world related to my business... "

B. M., Entrepreneur

CHAPTER NINE

Coping With External Forces

*All of us are a great deal more
than the sum of our academic years,
credentials and experience.
We are, in fact,
a composite of internal talents
and abilities which are both inborn
and developed over the years.*

◆ Factors Which Reduce Freedom in Career Choice

For those of you who are wrestling with career decisions or are simply caught in an untenable situation without a visible way out, there are a number of general forces which make career decision making difficult. The solution is to nullify the effect of these forces. That can be done only by stark self-honesty, which is difficult for any of us, and particularly so without adequate support and guidance — which many of us may be unwilling to seek.

It requires a special effort for us to unlock ourselves from all the forces which have accumulated over the years, to overcome the fear of rejection, boldly choose what we really want to do, and then move confidently, professionally, and effectively within the market in any chosen direction and achieve a predetermined goal. Once met, however, this is the most satisfying challenge of all.

Let's take a closer look at those factors that can make career decision making difficult:

◆ Cultural Forces Reduce Freedom of Career Choice

In the United States, we have allowed cultural forces to encroach on our freedom. It is a very subtle force which operates on all of us.

We have freedom of speech, of assembly, of religion — freedoms for which we are envied throughout the world. We make hundreds of choices a week about various things from buying and selling, to family projects, to relationships with friends and business associates, and countless other activities. Paradoxically, however, we rarely, if ever, use this freedom to make decisions about our careers.

Cultural forces — including our legal heritage, the pioneer spirit and the general work ethic of our country — have contributed to this reluctance to exercise freedom of choice. It is the nature of governments to control and the nature of people to want to be reasonably supported but not controlled. The control by our government is hidden behind the trappings of democracy, but we all know it is there. It controls our lives and careers. The government regularly surveys the work force and projects what is going to happen in the future, i.e., we need more (or less) people in a certain field. When such a report is made, it causes schools to emphasize, and people to start studying, the fields where need is said to be strongest. Then the area becomes flooded. This happened in the early '80s in the field of computers. The system encourages people to choose occupations based on society's needs, rather than their own.

England surely had its historical influence on us in our submission to social pressure in careers. Our law derived from the English Common Law. In an uneasy syncretism with democracy, our system subtly supports government as the replacement of the King of England.

Beyond that, societal attitudes undoubtedly transferred from England to the U.S. Several of my clients born and raised in England describe the "stiff upper lip" concept and the need for people, whatever their lot in life, to grin and bear it. Similar ideas have been expressed by clients native to South Africa and Australia.

The citizens of any country deriving from the British Empire seem to have this inbred attitude.

And this includes the United States. From the time the Pilgrims landed on Plymouth Rock, Americans have been expected to make do with what they had. The approved behavior was to bite the bullet and do whatever was necessary for survival.

As the pioneers moved westward, the "nose to the grindstone," "shoulder to the wheel" way of life grew stronger, and went on to be magnified out of proportion during the Depression. It was essential for people to hang on to whatever kind of job they had, no matter what it was, no matter how demeaning it was. The government started programs to help people survive, which created great dependence on the government.

An attitude has therefore been firmly established among us: If we do whatever fate has allotted us and if we do a good job, then somehow we will be rewarded. We should not promote ourselves, but rather wait for someone with authority to notice us and mete out the just rewards and punishments that are due. It became a cultural adage that we should not "toot our own horn." However, if we accept this approach to our personal careers, we deny our own personalities, our own hopes and aspirations, our own needs, and we live by someone else's.

> **When people take the initiative
> and wrestle through a personal career decision,
> their self-esteem and personal pride
> are unparalleled.**

Avoiding responsibility for our career decisions allows us to "buy into" a fatalistic attitude toward work. Whatever our family wished for us, whatever our schooling happened by chance to be, whatever our experience has been, we accept because it was allotted us by fate or divine intervention. If it is uncomfortable, we use a number of social justifications to ease the pain: We say, "It is a good job; it supports the family." "It gives me security." "Work isn't supposed to be enjoyable." "I have two days off a week and a vacation once a year." A teacher: "It's nice to have the entire summer off each year".

Every comedian gets around to some form of the old joke: "It's a lousy job, but I cry all the way to the bank." That line always elicits a response from any audience because it strikes a national nerve.

The solution to this societal and cultural pressure is for each of us to quietly, deeply and honestly reflect on the degree to which all of these forces operate within us. Forces which are unconscious in us reduce our freedom of choice, cause frustration and affect our personal lives and health. If we become conscious of those forces, then we can freely go along with them or freely oppose them.

The Eastern bloc countries wanted their freedom, got it, and later some said they were better off the way they had been because they were not ready to handle the freedom. Freedom to control their own lives is something people have to fight for and help other people fight for. If they give it up, they become more and more dependent and find it harder and harder to make a choice.

I find something analagous with my clients: The greater number of years they spend not making decisions about their careers, the harder it becomes to turn their lives around and regain control. However, when people take the initiative and wrestle through a personal career decision, their self-esteem and personal pride are unparalleled. They become vitalized and confident because they have taken control of their own destinies.

♦ Family and Early Life Experiences Limit Career Choice

As William Wordsworth put it, "The child is father of the man." My understanding of that line is that the conglomerate of activities, behavior, experiences and all forces operating on any of us when we are children shape what we are to become in adulthood. While hopefully a majority of those forces have a positive and beneficial effect, there are also those which have a lasting detrimental effect on the individual into adulthood.

Let's look at some of those specific forces that often restrict our freedom of choice. They subtly channel our thinking in certain directions, and reduce our ability to think beyond certain limits. All of this is linked with the cultural and historical elements discussed in the previous section, and with our education and work experience.

1. Family and Religious Principles and Forces.

The Modesty/Humility Syndrome. Most of us learn from early childhood, within the family circle, that we are to be modest and humble at all times. "The meek will inherit the earth," we are told, and we should never take the first place at the table, but rather the last. We overlook another seemingly contrary admonition that we are not to bury our talents in a field, but we are to use and multiply them. Our society's definition of humility seems to mean a lessening of self. On the contrary, real humility is truth. These attitudes, unidentified and unresolved, cause, or contribute to, a lack of self-esteem.

Specific Parental Values. Many values are implanted in our minds which we may never want to question since to do so might dishonor our parents. An exaggerated example: A client of some years ago grew up in a very strict religious atmosphere. He later became an atheist. He was obviously capable, but never excelled in his career. During a session in which we helped him examine attitudes remaining from childhood, he became suddenly silent and thoughtful and finally said, "I've just realized that I erased from my mind the fact that my father used to tell me that it was sinful to make any more money on a job than just enough to live on. I never wanted to believe that, but just now realized that for 15 years I have been unconsciously obeying my father." His income, in effect, had never been more than "just enough to live on."

Emphasis on Past Failures. The most common cause of an inferiority or guilt complex is a parent who never praises the children, no matter how well they do ("praise a child and you turn his head"), but always punishes them ("spare the rod and you spoil the child") when they fail to measure up. The only measure of self, therefore, that children have of themselves is parental attitude, expressed as a negative. In a milder form of this same attitude, we are taught from a very young age that we are supposed to learn from our mistakes. Nobody encourages us to learn from our successes.

Parental Favoritism. Sometimes a parent will appear to give more support to one child than to the other. The second may know intellectually that he or she is capable, but has a buried fear of being valueless and is forced to live with a crippling contradiction. The favored child, on the other hand, may be hampered by unidentified feelings of guilt.

It is a wonderful thing that we honor our fathers and mothers. However, when we hide behind it to avoid certain truths or to deny real resentments, it undermines our self-esteem.

2. Child Abuse.

Physical, mental or sexual abuse perpetrated on a young child can have lasting and devastating effect on self-esteem and consequently on career success. The solution, as always, is for the individual to come to grips with what in reality *did* happen, deal with the continuing effect (anger, humiliation) it has had on him or her, and gradually develop the realization that whatever it was need not have bearing on the value of the person today.

Denial or "voluntary amnesia" is a common human response to any form of abuse. The solution is to face the fact honestly, put it in perspective, and go on with our lives.

3. Role Models.

Most of us, consciously or unconsciously, pattern ourselves after (or against) certain people who have importance in our lives. The tendency to compare ourselves with others can be a self-diminishing exercise, because no matter how good we may be at a given ability, we can always find someone who is better.

The child is father of the man.

There are *positive* role models and *negative* role models — people whom we try consciously or unconsciously to be similar to, or different from. Whether this is conscious or unconscious, it reduces our freedom to be ourselves. A number of role model concepts can and do co-exist in our minds and can coalesce into a major force which keeps us from being what we truly are and from doing what we truly want to do.

4. The Family Business or Profession.

It is often said by people in their 40s and 50s that they wish they had never taken over the family business. Others wish they had never rebelled against it when they were young adults. Whether parents promote the idea or not, the existence of a family business is likely to reduce children's freedom of choice.

One of our most successful clients was a young man whose parents were teachers. His older brothers and sisters all succumbed to the parent's expressed desire that their children be teachers. This young man had never completed college because he knew if he graduated he would be under constant, subtle pressure to follow in his parents' footsteps. He harbored a deep resentment against both his mother and his father. Once he faced his resentment, he was able to decide on a career path.

He moved to another state to escape parental pressure and within two years, had founded three successful businesses.

In most families, there are certain ideas that are inadvertently implanted when we are young. It can be understood in individual families, for example, that children must become doctors, lawyers, dentists, teachers — all of these and more, singly or in combination. Women in general up to recent generations were expected to become housewives and mothers, teachers, nurses, secretaries, with perhaps a few other possibilities. Under this kind of "programming" it is difficult for a person to envision broader horizons.

◆ Education Limits Freedom of Career Choice

The U.S. education system is cited as the cause of many of the ills in our society. If that is true, then it should be no surprise that it would affect our career lives.

Among the most powerful forces limiting our choices in career, it is sad to say, is our education — the way it influenced us, the level of education we have, and the level we do not have.

First, let's look at a few considerations on how education influenced us from kindergarten through high school. There seems to be the general message for all students that, to be anything at all, it is necessary for each to go on to college. This message swells to a crescendo in the third and fourth year of high school when career planning courses intensify, vocational preference tests are administered, "college days" are held, aptitude tests are administered, and students' mail boxes are filled with mailings from colleges around the country.

All of this implies that without college, the student will have difficulty getting and holding a job and making good money. As a result, many students go to college who would be better advised to get some work experience immediately.

Students who, for one reason or another, cannot go directly on to college are made to feel ignored, diminished and of less value, and are more likely to fail. Few in the system seem to know how to teach a high school student to make a living without a bachelor's degree.

College students will be encouraged to take some vocational preference tests to determine what course of studies might be most appropriate. Unfortunately, since the preference tests compare students' input with those of people in given occupational fields, entering one of the indicated fields will bring about a strong likelihood that the choice will be unsatisfying.

The reason: About 90 percent of the workforce in any field are themselves not satisfied with their careers. At the very least, the use of such tests creates a dependency on their results and does not foment individual, independent decision making.

Oftentimes, there is the chance remark by a professor which persuades the impressionable student to pursue a certain course of study. An advisor may note the student is good at physics and suggest physics and engineering go well together. The student may jump at engineering simply because there are no other possibilities in mind.

That brings us to the level and kind of education we have and what it does to us. If, through questionable decision-making processes, you become a doctor, lawyer, dentist, educator, engineer, physician, etc., then it can become embarrassing to entertain the thought that perhaps you would rather do something else. Our degrees, our years in school, the grades we earned, all become part of that battery of credentials which form our ego foundation: As we were formed in school, so are we now, and so must we remain forevermore.

The higher the educational degree, the more entrapped the person who has earned it becomes. The person with a degree has an ego foundation so powerful that it might be perceived as more painful to leave the now undesirable field than to live with it. Employers will not give credit for anything beyond the scope of the degree. (What else could a lawyer or a minister do?) Often, people with degrees in, say, history, English, or the humanities, feel that their schooling was impractical. Perhaps it wasn't even worth the effort. What they have, they feel, is not "marketable."

There looms in the minds of all of us the question whether at any given moment we have either enough education or the right kind of education to promote our own causes.

A person without a college degree generally feels that he or she can have no real future beyond humdrum tasks which are relatively low paying. There is an internal, pervasive question: "Why try? They (employers) won't want me anyhow."

People with a master's degree, and particularly with a doctorate, can feel almost encased in concrete in their field of concentration. In some unspoken way they, too, become victims of the "just-a" syndrome. We've heard it from everyone: I'm just a housewife, what else can I do? I'm just a lawyer ... I'm just a broadcaster ... I'm just a teacher ... I'm just an engineer ... I'm just a school administrator ... and on and on and on.

The automatic reaction, inculcated in school, when a person feels driven out of a field either by personal dissatisfaction or by external circumstances, is to go back to school "to learn another skill." Therefore many people in their 30s, 40s and 50s, not knowing what else to do, will immediately go to school, pick a course of study, and then find that the standard job-hunt methodology works against them: They are too old to be considered for a trainee position (and frequently the pay would not support them) and they are too inexperienced to be considered for any other position. It's a classic Catch-22.

The automatic reaction ...
when a person is driven out of a field ...
is to go back to school "to learn another skill."

The only way out of this, of course, is for all of us to realize that we are a great deal more than the sum of our academic years and credentials. In some cases we may be something entirely different than our credentials might suggest. We are in fact, a composite of internal talents and abilities which are both inborn and developed over the years.

The self-esteem and self confidence required to act on that realization can only be developed when we openly perceive the limitations placed upon us and achieve the freedom to make our own personal decisions relating to life and career.

◆ Fighting the Education System

Many years ago, a man came to me for counseling who had himself been a counselor — a guidance counselor in a local public school system. We took him through a number of exercises designed to help him determine what his true needs and talents are and then explained the goal-setting process that would allow him to more fully take charge of his career.

At the end of our session, he looked at me and said, "I guess we've been doing it backwards all these years. We've been telling them what to do instead of letting them make their own decisions."

"We" in this case is our country's educators. "Them" is the millions of students whose career paths are indelibly influenced by their educational experiences.

No doubt about it: Education as it's now construed contributes as much to inappropriate career decisions as any other factor. For the most part, our schools don't help with career decisions — they program. And many of us spend the rest of our lives either succumbing to or fighting that programming.

Let me be clear that I am not at all opposed to tests and grading systems as means of motivation, encouragement, and discipline, and of ascertaining whether a student has learned the given material. What I am opposed to is that the system in which people who score well on tests in certain areas are automatically pushed to pursue further training and careers in those areas. The problem, of course, is that just about anyone can study hard and do well on a test, regardless of like or dislike of the subject matter. This is especially true of our top students.

In fact, I once worked with a young woman — a high school senior — who was being encouraged by the school to go into math and science because she got straight A's in those subjects, even though they were fields in which she was definitely not interested. She had a flair for these subjects and an ability to score well on related tests, but she also had a strong artistic bent and a people-orientation.

Eventually, her parents asked us to help her examine her interests and feelings. After that, her parents were able to help her counter the school's influence.

The effect was startling. Within weeks, she had laid out what amounted to a plan for her life. Her entire attitude became much more positive.

The next flaw in the system is that teachers in specific areas project their biases to their students. I suppose it is human nature for a teacher to encourage his or her best students to pursue careers in the area that he or she teaches, but that does not make it right. The correct thing is to take into account the individual human factors that are so important in making the right career decisions.

Lastly, there is an ingrained methodology of school guidance that's used because "that's the way it's always been done." It is based on how students perform on psychological and preference tests and how they appear to certain teachers. Perhaps worst of all, it centers around a supposedly empirical assessment of what the "hot" careers are going to be ten years from now.

We must face it: It does not matter what the hot careers are going to be in ten years. Someone who was not right for computer programming ten years ago probably still is not right for it today. But you can bet there are a lot of unhappy people in that field who went into it because some guidance counselor somewhere convinced them there was a "great future" in it.

The fact is, *any* career choice made on the basis of an objective assessment of your talents, needs and desires has a great future in it. Unfortunately, helping students make such an assessment is not something in which our educational system has ever developed its expertise.

And what does all this mean to you? For one thing, I hope you will bear all this in mind when it comes time to talk to your own children about career choices. And students, get all the input you need from those who know you and love you, but make your own decisions based on an objective assessment of your own hopes, aspirations, talents, and values.

It is crucial that everyone, especially those who are experiencing any kind of unhappiness in your career, examine the entire issue of undue influence applied by external forces — perhaps especially those implanted in you by your education.

♦ College Degree vs. Career Choice

You have to give the American education establishment credit: It has managed to inculcate the business establishment and the American people with the ideas that you *must* go to college straight out of high school because you cannot get a decent job without a college degree.

Businesses have by and large perpetuated this myth by tacking "college degree required" onto almost every job listing, then shortsightedly rejecting applicants who do not have degrees.

However, is the candidate who missed graduating from Harvard by one class credit any less qualified than the candidate with the bachelor's degree from one of our local institutions? Of course not. How about the candidate who missed graduating from Harvard by three credits? By six credits? By nine credits? Where is the line, if there is one?

Viewed in this light, a college degree is a fairly arbitrary measure of whether a person is qualified for a particular position. This is not to say that a college education is undesirable or unnecessary, but the notion of "getting a degree" seems to have superseded the importance of making a free choice with regard to career.

The subject is important. Many people, perhaps feeling a bit down after losing or leaving a job, seem to conclude that the solution to their problems is to "go back to school."

The notion of "getting a degree" seems to have superseded the importance of making a free career choice.

This is more a tribute to the marketing job done by the education establishment than a viable solution to *any* problem. Education marketers have convinced us that if we do not know what we want to do, we should just go to school.

This cannot work. Education in such instances is a path of least resistance that makes it easy to put off tough choices about career. And usually when people make those tough career choices, they find that more college education isn't the answer.

Among several thousand of my clients, only two went back to school immediately after setting career goals — one because the technical nature of his choice required it and the other, simply because he had the time, the money, and the inclination to do so.

Granted, there are those people for whom the pursuit of education is a career path in itself — historians and writers for example — but for most people, college must be treated as a means to an end, with one of the ends being a career goal.

The problem here, of course, is that we expect everyone to know by the age of 18 exactly what career to pursue. We give students little help in making that decision beyond some fairly dreadful vocational preference tests.

A far better way to go about it, in many cases, is for people to work or travel for awhile after graduating from high school, then go on to college if they so decide and if they have a career goal that can be furthered by a college education. To accomplish this, high schools must do a far better job of preparing a student to cope with life.

This is (or was) a fairly common practice in Europe, and it seems to be widely acknowledged that European education systems are currently superior to America's. Americans are pushed to go to college, where they're subject to the pressure of parents, professors and counselors trying to decide for them what they should do. Then, with degree in hand, they feel compelled to pursue a career in their major (especially if the education marketers have been successful in getting them to pursue an advanced degree) since, after all, an education is a substantial investment and we Americans believe in protecting our investments.

It all comes back to the notion that you're not qualified unless you have a degree. It just is not so.

Employers want people who will solve problems and provide assistance toward greater productivity and profit, not the person who has the most impressive degree from the most impressive school. While many qualifiers must be added, life experience as a learning factor related to the world of work is far more valuable than any amount of time spent in a classroom.

In fact, one of the smartest, most successful people I have met was a Chicago businessman who had never gone past the second grade. He used to delight in his "uneducated bumpkin" image and would even play up to it by pretending not to understand certain words. But I would pit his knowledge (and his incredible vocabulary) against that of any MBA anywhere.

Another former client was a man who, at age 14, had been set up in his own small business by his parents. He sold the business when he graduated from high school and was so far ahead of his classmates in terms of his business knowledge and decision-making capability that there was simply no comparison.

Rather than going to college, though, he went to work at a higher-than-usual rung of the field he had decided to enter, worked his way up for five years, *then* went to college to strengthen his career. He was a chief executive officer by the time he was 30, and I doubt that anyone has ever asked him about his degree.

There's no doubt that a college education can broaden your mind and develop your abilities to think and reason — abilities that can be applied to many fields. But let's keep things in perspective: Career choice should come first. Education should support it.

Perhaps as many as 99 percent of careers commence with a series of accidental circumstances.

◆ Work Experience Reduces Career Vision

Among the various factors which reduce our freedom to choose the course we would like our career lives to take, the final one is the actual work experience we have had over the years. Experience is a problem in three ways: 1.) It determines the way others view us. 2.) It limits the way we view ourselves. And 3.) It causes conditioned reflexes or "molding processes" in each of us by means of prolonged repetitive activities in a given field and/or type of work.

Let's consider each of these problems.

1. The Way Others See Us.

Perhaps 99 percent of careers commence with a series of accidental circumstances.

For example, if a person is born into a family in which there is a family business, then the children may be expected to carry on the family tradition. This is a natural hope of the parents, and can be easily understood by the children to be their destiny. Such a person is generally perceived by others as going into the family business and is not expected to aspire to anything else.

Oftentimes a person will feel compelled to stay with the major studies acquired in college. Our college degree and the studies which were part of it become our "ego foundation" — the way we view ourselves and the way others perceive us.

In many cases, a career pattern is set by some accident immediately after school. In need of a first job, the new graduate with a degree in political science may be referred by a friend to the heavy equipment company on the other side of town; after a few years in heavy equipment, such an individual is perceived as an industrialist, in spite of the political science major. On the other hand, a young graduate with a degree in business may be referred to a necessary first job in City Hall — and thus begins a long political career.

Typically, none of the people in these examples will be given credit for abilities beyond the field each is identified with. The general message we receive from organizations is that we must have a certain number of years of experience in a field and be a certain age if we are to be considered for a given position. Another message is that we cannot reach a top manager's position unless we started 30 years ago as he or she did in the mail room of the company (or some other beginning level of responsibility).

The only solution is to take a good look at the talents which are within us which make countless alternatives possible, and be prepared to be more than competitive in the job market.

2. The Way We See Ourselves.

Following the dictates of our society, we see ourselves as historical "tools" who have performed a number of functions for our employers. Whenever we look for another job, we automatically consider the number of companies we have worked for and enumerate and evaluate the different jobs we have held within each one.

The resume each of us is expected to write, analogous to a photograph, simply freezes us in place; neither resume nor photograph will show the animation and the breadth of activity that the individual is capable of. Our vision is therefore restricted to the past. If I have been a millworker, then I am hard pressed to think of myself in any other terms. If I have been working in purchasing for a number of companies, if I have been doctor, lawyer, banker, accountant, technician, etc., then I feel I can be nothing other than what experience has molded me into. Whatever we have done is something we can certainly do again, and a potential employer is likely to reject us if we can't show the required years of experience.

3. Our Conditioned Reflexes.

Each occupational grouping develops its own habit patterns formed from the "way things are done" in that industry. Military officers work in a unique setting - its closest approximation in civilian life being a police force. Bankers develop yet another set of work habit patterns. Retail store managers yet another. And so on. Each occupational grouping operates differently. Beyond that, each person — depending on personality, type of companies worked in, types of bosses, etc. — will develop unique patterns. It's as if each person adjusts to a subculture and has never examined the differences between various occupations to determine what "cultural" adjustments might permit a transfer from one to another.

**Becoming something other than
the sum of our historical activities
is among the most difficult, necessary
and refreshing challenges which face any of us.**

An accountant of 20 years' experience perceived himself as reserved and introverted. In reality, his personality was outgoing, extroverted and socially bold. The type of work he did, his "conditioned reflexes" in effect, left him with an inaccurate image of himself. Whenever our work dominates our lives, this kind of warped self-understanding is entirely possible for any of us.

Historical activities pile up behind us. The list of organizations we have worked for becomes longer and longer. The actual responsibilities we have are repeated for years. The walls we put around the "box" we are in, both in our own minds and in the minds of others, become thicker and thicker. As the years go by, it becomes increasingly difficult to be flexible and base our career futures upon the real talents and the real hopes and aspirations that dwell within us.

Becoming something other than a computer card, or a numbered functionary, both in our own minds and in the minds of others, is among the most difficult, yet necessary and refreshing challenges which face any of us. This is the way to a truly competitive stance in the marketplace and to true freedom in our career choices.

♦ Vocational Preference Tests

This section is not so much about vocational preference tests as it is about why they are a form of institutional cruelty which has been foisted upon us by otherwise well-meaning individuals.

I was first prompted to write about vocational preference tests after a ninth-grader I knew took a widely used test developed by a well-respected institution of higher learning. The test, which consists only of 20+ questions (hardly in-depth), indicated that she was cut out to be a painter, a floor and carpet layer, a heavy equipment operator, a baker, a rotary driller, a parole and probation officer, a coach and recreation director, or a firefighter.

Of course, she did not *want* to be any of these things and she was bright enough to ignore the test results. But many people, especially teens, no matter how bright they are, do not. Instead, they start amassing experience in the field that the test says they should be in and if things don't work out, they simply blame the test — or themselves.

Supporters of vocational preference tests claim they are only "idea" starters or "guides" or "suggestions." Such words, however, are meaningless to teenagers or vulnerable adults. As far as these people are concerned, the test has come to a conclusion for them and they cannot be expected to interpret it any other way.

Letting tests make your decisions for you is absolutely no way to approach your career.

Americans in general have become too dependent on *things* and *other people* making their decisions for them. We have a tendency to neatly analyze things and put them in boxes. We avoid hard choices such as those that are necessary to carve out a successful career path. Vocational preference tests are another example of the American way.

But letting a test make your decisions for you is absolutely no way to approach your career. A story I have used before helps to illustrate the point:

A national study of more than 1,000 nurses found that some 90 percent of them were unhappy with their careers. Now, suppose you took a vocational preference test and after matching your answers with the common denominators of people in the nursing profession, the computer determined that you "should" be a nurse. The test would be steering you toward a career in which you would have a nine in ten chance of being unhappy — just like nurses. It just doesn't make sense.

Here's another case in point:

A teenager was told by a vocational preference test that he was well-suited to be a funeral director. Because there is good money in that field, his parents began pushing him towards it. Prior to that time, he had given no thought to being a funeral director. In fact, if he had been asked if he wanted to be one, he'd probably have answered a flat "No." But because of a test, his answers, which may have been formed by his mood or by social forces and parental pressures, suddenly stripped him of an element of free will. It's frightening. (This is not meant as a slap at funeral directors. All of the funeral directors I know are outstanding people who truly love their work and the vital service they provide.)

Good career consultants have horror stories to tell about people who were misled by these tests. Yet the popularity of these tests grows and now we find them rearing their ugly heads at high school freshmen. Avoid these tests. If your children are subjected to them, urge them to ignore the results (or at least not take them as an end-all conclusion) and to make their own decisions.

I suppose vocational preference tests can help someone get at who they really are and what they really want, or be a means of identifying strengths and weaknesses, but there are definitely better ways of doing it.

The most important idea that I can leave with you is that career decisions must be made by *you*, the individual, based on awareness of your own needs and talents. No one else, no thing, no test, can make that decision for you.

**If a person is to be truly "self-directed"
in life, career, and job,
there is required a complete reversal
of the attitude and method instilled in us by society.
Instead of a passive role
in which employers are permitted
to examine and evaluate one's background,
there is required the eminently *active* role
in which a person communicates,
not what he or she has done somewhere else ...
but internal talents and abilities
as they pertain to a given situation.**

"It really is possible to do <u>anything</u> you want ... "

P. J. G., Entrepreneur

CHAPTER TEN

Solutions

A valid career is dynamic.
It grows with the individual.
It changes as the person
and society change.

◆ The Career Check-Up

Regular check-ups are a part of life for most of us. We do not wait until we are ill or bleeding to see the doctor, nor do we wait until our teeth ache to see the dentist. Ideally, we get regular check-ups to keep ourselves healthy.

When it comes to career however, a regular check-up is almost unheard of. Instead, people wait until a devastating malady befalls them (i.e., they get fired or chronically depressed) before seeking a remedy.

This is sad. Regular career check-ups would save many people a great deal of misery and would probably make our entire society happier and more productive.

Once a year, at least, you should give yourself a career check-up. It simply means spending a day or two taking a long, hard look at your current career situation and asking yourself some tough questions.

In most cases, it's best to do this with a spouse, a close friend, or a professional consultant who can help develop some objective insights. The ego identification we have with our careers often makes it hard to be honest with ourselves.

First, ask yourself if you're really growing or if your career has developed into a static situation. Personal growth is defined differently by each of us, but in general we are growing when we are challenged and are learning things that contribute to our overall career goals. If, upon introspection, you find that your job has become a dull routine, it may be time to move on.

Second, ask yourself if a decision you made when you were 18 years old dominates your career to this day. Over the course of time, our priorities change and we recognize needs in ourselves that we might not have recognized when we launched our careers at the age of 18. At that age, many people just need a job. Any job. Your needs are likely to go on to become far more complex.

Of course, there are some people who have never bothered to define what their needs are at all and therefore might not be able to answer this question. These people have some extra work to do.

Third, ask yourself if you're developing habit patterns that restrict your vision. Years of performing a certain function will cause you to adopt a way of thinking and acting that affects your attitude toward life and career. I have found this to be especially true among teachers, lawyers, and police and military officers. People who can think beyond their habit patterns are the ones who usually stand out in their fields.

Fourth, ask yourself if you are as decisive as you were a year ago. You probably will need the help of a spouse, friend, or professional for this one. If not, it could be because career issues — overt or subconscious — are clouding your mind.

Fifth, ask yourself if you are as capable of taking a calculated risk as you were before you started your present job. For many of us, the accumulation of material things and the need to maintain them force us to play it safe, or at least force upon us the perception that we must play it safe. Even if a mortgage is forcing you to stick with something unsatisfactory, it's healthier to admit that you do not like it than to pretend you do.

Sixth, ask yourself if you are more comfortable or less comfortable with other people than you were a year ago. When we are discontented with our careers, we tend to become more reclusive. Perhaps a feeling of shame is associated with what we are doing.

Finally, ask yourself if things could be better. The answer is *always* yes. The steps you need to take to make those improvements could seem unimportant — installing new lighting in the office perhaps — or they could call for a major career move into another field. It's like marriage. If two people have a great relationship, but don't work at improving it, it will go downhill. And the characterization is appropriate: You are married to your career.

To return to the earlier analogy, people often avoid going to the doctor when they sense something is wrong because of fear of what the doctor might tell them. A similar thing happens in career. People will blithely slide through life telling themselves everything is fine when in fact everything is not.

In our society today, entire industries are becoming obsolete while new industries rise to dominate the economic scene. Everyone should be ready to capitalize on the possibilities by carving out a personal vision. Start with a career check-up.

◆ Reclaiming Self-Esteem on the Job

If we believe statistics, it is fair to say that a good number of us are suffering from low self-esteem, and our low self-esteem is a direct result of our job or career decisions. Ongoing studies continue to say that 80 to 90 percent of us do not like the work we are doing. If those studies are correct, then no matter what type of work we accept, we have a four out of five chance of being unhappy. This dissatisfaction leads to an intense kind of stress that permeates all other aspects of our lives and results in low self-esteem.

The work ethic that has been ingrained into each American has come into direct conflict with the realities of the rapidly changing work environment of the '80s and '90s. Businesses are down-sizing, entire industries have become obsolete, and other industries that did not exist ten years ago have arisen and become dominant.

Responsibilities attached to certain jobs have changed. How many of us were using computers in our work ten years ago? How many of us can even guess what kind of skills we will need ten years from now? These kinds of stresses did not exist 70 or 60, or even 30, years ago when jobs and companies changed very little, if at all.

> **We identify and refer to ourselves
> by the type of work we do.
> If we do not like our work,
> we cannot like ourselves.
> The result is low self-esteem.**

We now know that jobs and companies change dramatically. Unfortunately, the stick-with-it-no-matter-what work ethic has not changed. The result is low self-esteem.

Career and job have become our ego foundations. We identify and refer to ourselves by the type of work we do. As such, if we do not like our job or our work, we wind up not liking ourselves. We lose belief in ourselves and in our ability to do whatever we put our mind to. The result is low self-esteem.

There are some other tangible causes of stress and resulting loss of self-esteem. First and foremost is dissatisfaction with the current situation. Everybody, of course, experiences short-term dissatisfaction, from things like an argument with the boss, the addition of responsibilities, etc., and these come and go. It's the long-term dissatisfactions that must be faced squarely, but rarely are.

Job loss, of course, is a rather obvious cause for loss of self-esteem, even if the job loss is due to circumstances beyond the control of the individual, as it often is in this era of "down-sizing." Loss of job translates into loss of ego.

Changes within a company — attitudes, management styles, expansion, down-sizing — all of these can cause stress.

Finally, changes in ourselves cause stress. People somehow never stop to consider the fact that they change even if their jobs and careers do not, and these changes create intense stress. It's not at all unusual in our society to see a 50-year-old whose career is simply the result of decisions made when he was 18. But more often than not, we ignore the changes in ourselves and buckle under to the social pressure to conform and be "a good provider."

We all have freedom of choice.
But the choice made in career oftentimes
is not to exercise that choice.

We as a society have chosen to deal with the symptoms, rather than the causes of our career stress. We run, we pump iron, we take valium. After all, we are Americans. We chop down trees, we build log cabins, we survive harsh winters. We can tough out anything that's thrown at us, including loss of self-esteem.

The point is that we all have freedom of choice. But the choice we most often make is to not exercise that freedom. We make hundreds of decisions *within* our jobs every day, but rarely do we make decisions *regarding* our job or career. We cave in to that peculiarly American machismo that dictates that we must be happy with our position — no matter what it is — as long as we get that paycheck and the two days off a week and two weeks off a year.

There is only one way to reclaim self-esteem on the job, and that is by taking charge of your career. Decide what you really want to do, then go out and do it. Do not allow your actions to be guided by the pressures of family or society. Don't be lulled into a false sense of security by a paycheck and your employer's "stability."

You are an individual with unique needs and talents, and it is your needs and talents, not your job, that define who you are. If your self-esteem is high, congratulations. You are one of the fortunate few. I hope you enjoy it and maintain it. If your self-esteem is low, look within. It is only there that you can reclaim what is rightfully yours.

◆ Making the Most of Personal Time

Is there a correlation between how we use our personal time and career satisfaction? The answer is undoubtedly yes. Somewhere along the line someone determined that if you spend too much time on the job and not enough time on yourself, you reach a point of diminishing returns. That's why we (theoretically) balance our days between work and leisure. We all need to address the question of where that balance is for ourselves. Where is that point of diminishing returns?

This subject comes up because, as part of my career counseling program, I ask people about their hobbies and leisure activities. Such activities are a very concrete clue to where a person's true talents and abilities lie, since few of us spend our free time doing those things we do not enjoy or are not good at.

However, many people who have become unhappy in their careers have let their hobbies decline. They become "couch potatoes," a term that has become something of a joke in our society but which, in my opinion, underlies a serious dissatisfaction with life and, more specifically, with one's job.

Not only are hobbies a clue to innate talents, the lack of hobbies is indicative of career problems.

Now there are those of us who spend 13 or 14 hours a day on the job and who protest that we have no time for hobbies or personal interests. While there are, no doubt, people who genuinely need to spend that much time at work, I suspect a far greater number who do so simply might not be capable of handling their workload in a more reasonable time or have allowed themselves to become unreasonably overtaxed.

In either case, it's a formula for disaster. To focus myopically on our jobs is to lose our personal identity. Even if you love your job, you still need to find hobbies that take your mind away from it, and you still need to find time for vacations.

The number of people I meet who tell me they have not taken a vacation in five years is astonishing. And they say so with great pride! Vacations are not a luxury; they are, rather, a necessity. Smart employers should *require* that their employees take vacations.

People also need to think in terms of personal growth outside the job. This can take two forms: One is self-improvement via community college courses or ongoing professional training. People who do not want to take the time to improve the skills they use on the job should seriously question whether they are on the right career path.

This need not necessarily mean taking classes directly related to what you do all day. They could be classes that are only peripherally related or that will give you skills that could make you more valuable to your employer.

It is important to think about personal growth, not only in career and job, but also *outside* the job — in other words, in the entire complex of our lives.

The second avenue to personal growth is taking the experience you have gained in your vocation and applying it to an avocation. Again, if you find this too distasteful to consider seriously, you might be in the wrong job. This is not to suggest that you should find some way to do in your spare time exactly what you do on the job. But it's possible to find connections between the two.

For instance, one of my clients is in the public relations field, a field that requires strong writing and verbal communication skills. As he honed these skills on the job, he was able to transfer them to his spare time, writing plays and acting with a number of area theater companies.

In other words, the skills he developed on the job were applied to his spare time, where they were honed even further and then reapplied to his job.

Things do not always work in such perfect harmony, of course. Another client with whom I worked many years ago was a heavy-equipment operator. In his spare time, he was an accomplished artist who produced magnificent oil paintings.

The bottom line is that for any of us to be truly happy with our careers, there must be a balance between work, hobbies and self-improvement. That balance will be different for each of us and we cannot look to someone else to tell us what it is. Rather, it's something we must find ourselves. It's well worth the effort.

◆ Selecting a Career Consulting Service

The time will come when it will be routine for people to seek outside professional help for the solution of career concerns as it is now to seek medical or legal support. If a career is perceived as being very important in our lives, then it makes sense to regularly seek professional career advice.

But caution is in order. Since about 1980 or before, there have been occasional news stories on a national scale about crackdowns on unscrupulous employment agencies and career consultants.

In any profession, of course, you will find con artists who prey on the unsuspecting for the sole purpose of bilking them out of their money. Whether it's a quack who offers a cancer cure, or a "career consultant" who promises to find a job for someone, charlatans will always pounce on people looking for an easy way out and willing to spend lots of money to get it.

In the cases recounted in the news, so-called placement firms took money from their victims — sometimes as much as $6,000 or more — promising to find jobs for these people. Shoddy resumes and outdated lists of corporate contacts were about all most of these firms could offer.

How can you protect yourself? Primarily by being aware of the many danger signals disreputable firms send out and knowing what to look for in a reputable firm.

First realize that there is no easy way to make a career move. It requires a lot of hard work; hard work that only *you* can do. Someone who implies that it will be easy or that they can do it for you should be severely questioned.

Next, if someone implies or claims to have access to the "hidden job market," turn tail and *run.* Yes, indeed, there *is* a hidden job market. Eighty percent to ninety percent of all jobs are filled without ever being advertised or listed with agencies. An expert career consultant can show you how to tap into that market and uncover those jobs, but there's *nobody* who has access to very many of them.

Now, if you determine that you need professional help with your career (other than the help available from an employment agency and search firm, which will match your background to available openings), **recognize that there are basically four types of career consulting services.**

First is the type which focuses on the practicalities of interviewing techniques and writing resumes, but offers no or little help in the areas of reassessment, planning, and career choice.

Secondly, there seems to be a fairly large number of counselors and counseling psychologists who have endeavored to expand their practices by offering "career counseling." There are many good counselors who can help people deal with the trauma of recent career experiences, but it is the rare one who can help an individual with an assessment of personal "marketability," provide the support and direction for a valid career choice, and give in-depth instruction on professionalism in business, career and job interview communication techniques.

Thirdly, there are firms which seem to restrict their activities to two areas: Career reassessment (for example, examining recurring job difficulties) and obtaining the next job (with emphasis on the practicalities of job interview techniques and resumes). To me, this is something of a "modified placement" firm, because so many of their clients end up with the same kind of job they had before — just a different setting.

A fairly recent client of mine worked with a local career consulting firm (now out of business) in the early '80s. He approached the firm with the intention of changing his career field. For a hefty fee, they "helped" him realize that the field was not his problem, but simply the firm he was involved with. In about three weeks' time, he took a position in another firm in the same field. About five years later, he came to us and finally got his wish: After *many* weeks and lots of work on both his part and our part, he changed to a different field.

Lastly, there is the full-service firm, which combines the offerings mentioned above, but takes a step further by helping the individual examine his or her real talents and needs, and make decisions about career direction, and by teaching professional methods of penetrating the marketplace. The *core* issue for such consultants is helping the individual make a valid *decision* about his or her career future. The procedure first *leads up* to that decision (personal reassessment, professional planning), then it *deals with* the decision (examining the market, considering options), and finally *follows upon* the decision (developing complete professionalism in market penetration).

As in everything else, it is important to realize that if you are dealing with honest professionals, you generally get what you pay for. Professional practitioners will charge within the local boundaries for hourly professional rates. If you want to be coached to handle a scheduled job interview, it can probably be done in two to ten hours, depending on the nature of the interview and the job. If you want therapy for recent (or long-term) traumatic career experiences, you may well be charged on an hourly basis for as long as you and your counselor determine is necessary. The more expert career counselor can command a higher rate. The more complete and supportive the service, the more hours involved.

Generally, we find that when people come to career consultants, they really do not know what they need for their careers. It's pretty much the same when we go to a physician or a lawyer: We want to find out what we need. Get a few opinions and you'll begin to know.

Once you start shopping around for a career consultant, it should be to determine what ranges of service are available, what is pertinent to your current needs, and where you can have the kind of relationship which will be productive for you.

Ask how long the firm has been in business. I do not want to suggest that a newcomer to the market cannot do an excellent job for you, but someone who has been in business for ten years is more likely to be legitimate than someone whose doors have been open only a few months.

Ask for references. While a reputable firm will not want to have its clients contacted indiscriminately, it should be willing to do so after preliminary steps permit you to say that you are seriously interested in the services.

Pay close attention to the degree to which the firm insists on individual responsibility. The more a firm promises to do your work for you, the less legitimate it is likely to be. Just as a doctor cannot "cure" you if you refuse to take your medicine, neither can a career consultant help you if you refuse to take charge of your own actions in a professional way.

Just as with most things, it's a matter of "buyer beware." But given the major role your career plays in your life, this is an area to which you should devote special concern.

It is important to realize that there is no easy way to make a career move. It requires a lot of hard work; work that only *you* can do.

"Here's what your program means to me: empowerment; taking control; career independence; learning the secrets that lead to personal and professional success; the secrets of human nature; the challenge of controlling the all-mighty interview; CEOs are only people; a systematic approach to success!"

M. B., Client

CHAPTER ELEVEN

Personal Professionalism

*The core quality of
the truly professional person
is empathy, which is
the most profound form of listening.*

◆ Professionalism Always Wins.

Current and recent events (the continuing recession, the breakup of the Soviet Union) have brought to mind a lesson learned nearly 20 years ago.

Many of us can still remember the time in 1973, when cars were lined up overnight to fill their tanks. Several times I took my own car in the evening to a gas station, locked it up and reluctantly left it until morning. During that period, my clients were more successful than were those I worked with prior to the gas crunch. I put the entire experience off as something of a fluke and was simply grateful that it had happened.

At the peak of that crisis, however, I learned the true explanation for the phenomenon. In a telephone conversation with a man who was in the auto sales and leasing business, I sympathized with him because I assumed that his business must be suffering from the economic situation. On the contrary, he told me, he was more successful than before. When I asked him how this could be, he said, "When times are good, any amateur can sell a car; when times get bad, the amateurs get out and leave it to the pros. If you know what you're doing, you can do well."

The parallel is obvious. When the economy is booming, anyone can get a job. When the economy goes sour, layoffs proliferate, unemployment rises, and it's difficult to get a job. But the person who moves into even a bad market with entirely professional methods can succeed where others will fail.

Several times during recessions since 1973, I have seen that same phenomenon — increasing effectiveness and a higher success ratio among my clients. The notable times were in 1981 and 1982, and now again in the 1990s. When a downturn is expected, employers are more reluctant to speak to anyone who appears to be looking for a job; they are frequently in some pain because they agonize over the necessity to lay off employees, and they worry about meeting expenses. At the same time, they have a business to run and they will respond to people who stand out as potential solutions and support systems. These thoughts suggest that we spend some time on the *benefits, results and effects* of professionalism.

Much has been spoken and written on the subject of professionalism, but invariably with reference to particular disciplines. For example, books are written (and professors spend time) on what it means to be professional in the practice of law, of medicine, in dentistry, etc.

There is a more fundamental concept: *Personal* professionalism. To function with true professionalism within a given discipline, in a career and in life itself, the individual must be professional *as a person*.

A professional person will quickly and accurately establish an appropriate career direction. Such a person will more surely obtain the series of positions and/or businesses which will be the sum total of a lifetime career. Truly professional persons, always improving themselves as "people relators," will with increasing competence relate to the bosses, subordinates and peers who will be part of their career lives as they move along their chosen track.

During the recession of the early '80s, when one of my clients first met with the employer who later hired him, he was immediately told that the company had not hired in months but had rather been laying off people in large numbers.

The message was clear: If you're looking for a job, you've come to the wrong place. Some weeks later, this client was hired and given the responsibilities of three employees who were laid off to make way for him. In the process, the employer saved about one-half of the total of the three salaries and gave the other half (a very substantial salary) to his new employee.

When times are bad, the usual answer for those who are unemployed is to work harder at making job-hunt contacts: Disseminate resumes, pursue want ads and register with employment agencies.

On the contrary, the only effective answer lies in working "smarter," not simply harder. In the truest sense, working smarter means working as an unqualified professional. It requires a complete "retooling": Taking charge of our own destinies instead of leaving our destinies to the way others (employers) perceive us. It means taking the attitudes which are part of our society and moving 180 degrees around the circle, from being a "job hunter" to becoming a person who makes planned and controlled moves toward a carefully established goal. The goal must be based upon the hopes, aspirations, talents, abilities, values, and convictions that live within each of us. Difficult? Of course it is. Because our system prepares us to be employees (subordinates), not active agents who control our own career destinies.

The only effective answer to unemployment is to work *smarter* in looking for work, not simply harder.

It requires an act of courage to modify these attitudes. But someone once said that most of the great things of this world are accomplished by people who are somewhat sick to their stomachs at the time. Or who have to swallow around the lump in their throats. I submit that it is much easier to bear with that knot in the stomach as we move toward a carefully planned potential solution, than with the knot in the stomach which comes from passively accepting a painful situation over which we exercise no personal control.

As we experience tough times economically, it is the professional person who will stand out in the crowd of those who, in standard fashion, are simply "job hunting" or who are using a number of amateurish "tricks" which are designed to gain attention.

♦ The Imaginative Job Search

Complete professionalism is the key to a successful job hunt. The approach must be professionally done, the interview must be professionally done, you must exude professional confidence, your appearance — both in dress and grooming — must be professional. But professional does *not* mean unimaginative.

Just as employers hire confidence, so are they drawn to imagination. Nonetheless, I am constantly shocked at the incredible lack of imagination people put into their job hunts. Even supposedly "creative" people seeking the most creative positions often make their approach with the dullest techniques. And it seems to be that the more educated and experienced people are, the less imaginative they tend to be.

Part of the problem, of course, is that the business community mindlessly perpetuates an unimaginative system. Look at a want ad or call a manager to ask if there are any positions open and what do you get? "Send us a resume."

Letter-and-resume (by which I mean job history) is an antiseptic approach that neither relates to the current problems of an employer nor lends itself to creativity. Of course there are people who artfully prepare their resumes with different typefaces or paper stocks, but it's still a recitation of where they worked and when they worked there — none of which is all that important to a potential employer.

Let's analyze what employers care about. They want someone who will fill a current need now and in the future. They want someone who will help them make a profit. They want someone who is confident. They want someone who will listen.

It is impossible to convey those qualities in a job history.

What to do then? The most important thing is to put yourself in the shoes of the person filling the position and relate to the *person* rather than the job.

Hiring decisions are made by PEOPLE, not by computers.

The core element of professionalism is empathy. That is, project your mind into the minds of those doing the hiring and demonstrate not merely that you speak their language or fit the job description, but that you can empathize with their daily concerns and anxieties. Catch their attention and *demonstrate* that you understand their concerns; it is not enough to simply tell them you do. If you want a sales position, show that you can sell yourself. If you want a customer relations position, show some human concern.

How you do it is up to you and must be considered on a case by case basis, but here is a fairly well known example that illustrates the point.

About eight or nine years ago, a Los Angeles advertising copywriter who was seeking to move to the Northwest approached several major ad agencies. He did so by placing a mannequin's arm in one of those long boxes used for long-stem roses and writing on it, "I'd give my right arm to work for you."

I doubt that I would ever recommend such a degree of flamboyancy, but you can see the point. Not only did this mailing get instant attention, it clearly demonstrated that the man possessed a degree of creativity that is highly sought by ad agencies.

Such an approach probably would be unacceptable, for example, at an accounting firm, but it is possible to approach an accounting firm with something more imaginative than a letter and resume. After all, if the only thing an accounting firm cares about is getting the person with the most extensive background, the hiring decision can be made by a computer. But hiring decisions are not made by computers; they are made by *people*. And as I said earlier, people are drawn to imaginative individuals.

Here is another case history that demonstrates incredible imagination:

A former client decided that there was one particular Seattle company for which he wanted to work. He launched an intensive program of research into the company, learning as much as he possibly could about it, including the fact that the CEO flew to New York every Sunday afternoon for a meeting with a branch office, and returned to Seattle the next evening.

This man booked himself on the same flight one weekend, then waited at the airport for the CEO to appear. When he did, this client got in line behind him at the boarding gate counter and requested a seat assignment right next to the CEO.

Not only did he have a guaranteed five-hour audience with the CEO, but thanks to his research, he was able to demonstrate a knowledge of the CEO's daily concerns that no intelligent or rational person could dismiss. He was hired within a couple of weeks of his return to Seattle.

An extreme case? Sure. An extraordinarily imaginative individual? You bet. Are you capable of similar initiative? I imagine you are. Just be sure it's professional.

♦ Professionalism:
The Essence of a Successful Career

Education and experience alone do not make a professional. You are a professional when you project a number of precise qualities which have been well developed and well integrated so that together they constitute a *personal state of mind*. It is a state of mind which allows your abilities, expertise, and strength of character to be on full display without constituting a threat or a source of discomfort to another. The qualities of professionalism are entirely acquired and can always be improved: Empathy, confidence, organized action, and personal style. Two of them are deeply internal to the professional person — empathy and confidence — while two are more externally perceptible — organized action and personal style.

Empathy: The core quality of professionalism and most deeply a part of our personal being is empathy.

It is the imaginative projection of your own consciousness into another person's mind — in career terms, into a company and its needs. As such it is the most profound form of listening. Etymologically it means to "feel with" another person. Not to feel sorry for another (sympathy), but to profoundly feel and understand the other person's point of view, convictions, philosophy, etc. To listen this intently requires great effort and a good deal of practice. It requires setting aside your own personal pride to the point where you can be truly sensitive to another person and understand (not necessarily agree with) his or her viewpoint. True respect for others requires a perception of their individuality, and understanding the ways in which each of us is *different* from all others. This is undoubtedly difficult, for it is easier to categorize others and deal with their similarities. We find it even more difficult to deal with the differences in *group* personalities; and perhaps we Americans have an unusual difficulty with this. Our reluctance to perceive cultural differences is the most important source of the "Yankee Go Home" epithet.

We respond most strongly and quite unconsciously to EMPATHY ... which requires strong *confidence* — and employers hire and promote confident people.

When a person is looking for a job, the standard recitation of background information is, by implication, an insult — as if to say, the employer's company closely resembles other companies which formerly employed you. It is accepted because this is the standard job-hunt system. But every company (just like every town, section of the country, culture) has its own "personality," goals, hopes, aspirations, and language. It is important to learn about them and adjust to them. We must identify what really *is* true about the organization, as opposed to what we *hope* or *expect* is true.

Confidence: A professional person displays an open-minded willingness to hear the thoughts of others and to project his or her own without being threatening. It includes a venturesome attitude, visible self-respect, and a carefully courteous form of tenacity.

We respond most strongly, perhaps quite unconsciously, to *empathy* — a sincere interest by others in us. But real empathy requires strong *confidence*, which is more readily perceived by others. Employers hire and promote confident people. We usually can appear confident only when our experience supports our application for a given job along the same line. If we can be confident about our ability to be successful in a given position, *even if we have no direct previous experience in that kind of responsibility,* we can be serious contenders, and we will be taken seriously.

Organized Action: Consistent marks of professional people are that their goals are clear, they are organized in their approach, precise in their methods, and they never fail to follow through on an activity once it has been initiated. Professional "self-marketers" will, in similar fashion, identify their precise goals, organize their approach to the companies involved, hone interview techniques and methods, and be carefully courteous in follow-up procedures. A professional will not play (or at least will not depend upon) the numbers game of responding to ads, disseminating resumes, and registering with agencies.

Personal Style: A professional realizes that human (and business!) relationships frequently develop or founder depending upon first impressions. The elements in personal style must be carefully nurtured and developed:

1. Imagination: An imaginative, courteous person is the one people like to get to know. Avoid the crowd of resume presenters and job hunters — your chances are better at the gambling tables. Approach the *person*.

2. Dress and Grooming: For interviews, wear a *suit* (men and women) which is in style but conservative in cut and color. (Women have more latitude than men in this regard.) Shoes must be of good quality and well cared for. Add elements of flair with color of shirt or blouse, tie, etc. Hair should be styled to suit the times and your age group. Avoid extremes; avoid drabness.

It is important to realize that the interview situation *requires* appropriate dress because of two very important benefits: It is a mark of respect toward the employer, and "dressing up" for an occasion helps us to be at our best. It has been frequently observed that, everything else being more or less equal, when two people approach an employer, one wearing a suit and the other nicely but casually dressed, secretaries and then employers will usually defer to the one wearing a suit. It is a good idea for anyone to take advantage of the conditioning in the workplace: Various shades of blue and gray, for men particularly, are evidence of money, wealth, power, and competence.

3. Correct Posture and General Conduct: A relaxed (and occasionally smiling) face, appropriate eye contact, and display of enthusiasm are vital. Enlist the aid of a friend or family member and/or mirror for self-critique and improvement.

When any of us enter an employer's office for an interview, we face three important obstacles: Our own nervousness, the furniture, and distance.

Nervousness causes most of us to put a great deal of energy into appearing not nervous. This means leaning back in the chair and crossing our legs. We succeed only in appearing disinterested. Office furniture is so constructed that when we lean back in the side chair, and the employer sits normally in his or her executive chair, the employer sits at a slightly higher elevation. This allows the employer to exercise a greater measure of control. The distance from interviewee to employer, if both sit back in their respective chairs, is between six and eight feet, and the two personal territories do not meet. This also gives greater control to the employer, whose office it is. In our culture, an acceptable distance for comfortable discussion between two people meeting alone is four to six feet.

These three obstacles (nervousness, elevation and distance) can be tempered by a simple maneuver: After shaking hands and before being seated, *move* the chair you are about to sit in forward so that it is close enough, if you want, to comfortably lean one forearm on the edge of the desk, and then assume a posture of leaning forward. In leaning forward, you *use* your nervous energy in a positive way, you appear interested, you will talk more directly and therefore more effectively to the employer, you will elevate your head approximately six inches (which sends an important subtle message of equality), and you will reduce the distance between you to approximately four to six feet. This approach should be rehearsed so that it becomes natural and comfortable.

It will help you to notice that the most engaging people we deal with are those who talk and listen to us with their entire bodies. And they maintain a comfortable kind of eye contact with us. It is important to realize that many people find direct eye contact embarrassing, to the extent that constant eye contact can become something of a battle and therefore, distracting. And yet if we avoid eye contact, we may be judged as less than direct and honest. A compromise usually works for most people: Keep moving your eyes within the triangle of cheekbone to cheekbone to middle of forehead, with an occasional glance directly into another person's eyes. This is well worth rehearsing until it becomes natural and comfortable. It is important to avoid looking off to the other person's side or at any other part of the person's anatomy — any of these can cause discomfort in another person, or be misinterpreted.

4. Voice: Properly modulated, regulated and inflected, our voices convey many unspoken messages. It is important to speak naturally, unaffectedly and comfortably.

Nervousness can lead us to speak too rapidly, and at too high a pitch. Or, aware of the problem, we might slow down and speak too ponderously. Again, enlist the help of someone and/or use a tape recorder for self-critique and improvement. Proper rehearsal helps us to relax and to be ourselves.

Observing and using these concepts out of a motivation of respect for and courtesy toward others allows for the development of the most professional form of human rapport. Their practice prepares us, both physically and mentally, for the best possible self-projection in an interview, *and they enable other people to be at their most receptive.*

These concepts are the direct antithesis to some rather awful business philosophies which some people seem to admire. There are those who seem to believe that the way to business success is to intimidate others. Books have been written on this subject. A fairly recent thesis appears to be that one must learn to swim with the sharks and become adept at their methods. It is, of course, true that we have the right to defend ourselves if someone attacks us. It is a good idea to understand the methods of the "sharks" so as to effectively cope with them. But it must be remembered that we only win a few *"battles"* with such means. The *"war"* is won only when a significant number of people want us to win, or are at least willing that we do so. We can elicit this kind of support only with a professional approach which includes empathy and sincere human respect and concern.

Professionalism always wins.

CHAPTER TWELVE

For Managers

*The interview should address
the <u>talents</u> of the candidate,
not his or her historical activities.*

A most important part of any career is the ability to relate to and effectively work with other people. The development of a manager's career (for example) depends in large measure on improving his or her ability to communicate with subordinates, peers and superiors.

Much can be written on this subject. The following sections are of great importance specifically to managers, though many points raised also can be appreciated by employees of all levels.

An interview should be
geared to the PERSON,
not toward a sterile analysis
or his or her historical activities.

◆ How to Conduct a Good Interview

Although this book focuses on the need for individuals to take charge of their careers and techniques for doing so, employers must also take some responsibility for learning how to hire the right people. That means really *learning* how to interview.

How often have you, as an employer, begun an interview with the somewhat lame statement: "Tell me a little bit about yourself"? If you're a typical manager, you've done it far too often, even if you've done it only once.

I'm convinced there would be a lot fewer firings, and ulcers and heart attacks if people were hired on the basis of ability and compatibility instead of the rather sterile basis of experience. And that can start — perhaps end — with conducting better interviews.

Unfortunately, most interviews consist of an employer reading the applicant's resume, then looking up across the desk and uttering the dread statement. Usually, the job applicant will merely repeat what's on the resume, which brings both parties right back to ground zero.

Resumes, of course, create a "non-human" basis for hiring (since, when you get right down to it, experience is really the least important factor in hiring) and create a rigid, uncomfortable atmosphere when they're used as a crutch in interviews.

Now read the next two sentences several times, and *remember* them:

An interview should *not* be geared toward finding the person with the most experience. An interview should be geared toward finding the person who is going to be most effective at doing what needs to be done and who will be compatible with you and your company in a work relationship *regardless* of experience.

You can find that person by doing the interview correctly.

First, you must create an atmosphere in which the interviewee can relax and be natural. People have a difficult time keeping their guard up when they're relaxed and they feel that they're really being listened to.

Second, go into the interview with a clear vision of where the company is going and what responsibilities need to be addressed, but without any preconceived notion of what type of experience is needed to carry out those responsibilities. It's always better to tailor a job to the right person than vice versa.

Third, ask open-ended questions that revolve around:

The interviewee's daily concerns and anxieties. We all have them. Are they the same as yours?

The interviewee's personal goals and future plans. Can this person accomplish what he or she would like at your company?

A belief system or overall philosophy that is compatible with the company's.

Also look carefully at whether the candidate has a clear fix on a career pattern or simply views what you have to offer as "just another job."

You'll never get at these issues by saying "I see you used to be executive widget washer at Podunk, Inc. Tell me what that involved."

Instead, try something like "Over the years, what has been the common denominator in the work you enjoyed? What has been the common denominator in the work you didn't enjoy?"

The answer should give you a pretty good handle on whether the candidate would be happy with what you have to offer.

Another good question is, "What might you have changed at your last job (or any position) that would have made it better?"

This will give you some insight into the candidate's daily concerns and anxieties, since the answer will relate to how those anxieties might have been addressed.

To get a fix on a person's belief systems, ask about the overall philosophical approaches of their previous employers and then ask how comfortable the individual was working within that philosophy.

Finally, there's, "Describe your ideal job." This will provide some insight into future plans.

Not only do these questions provide more insight into a candidate, they do so without revealing too much about your company or your opening, making it difficult for the candidate to simply tell you what he or she thinks you want to hear.

> **It is much more important
> to tailor the job
> to fit the candidate
> than to make the candidate
> fit the job description.**

Some other questions:

"What was the most important thing you did on a day-to-day basis? What was the least important?"

"How did you feel about having to ... [specific responsibility]?"

"What motivates you to get up in the morning and go to work?"

You needn't use these questions verbatim, but I do think everyone must develop questions that relate more to whether a job can fill a candidate's needs than to whether a candidate's specialized experience matches the job description.

A few years ago, a client of mine encountered a business owner, a publisher, who also knew how to interview. The owner had tried to sell his business, but was forced to repossess it when the buyer failed to make a profit. The owner was in the process of dissolving his corporation and cutting his losses when my client approached him.

A long-term government worker, my client brought with him

a battery of talents and experience which nicely complemented the publisher's knowledge and ability. Since they both knew the questions to ask, they quickly reached a meeting of minds, and rebuilt the business. My client more than doubled his income in his first year in his new job.

———————

◆ The Corporate Career Review

A few years ago, after a column of mine on the subject of outplacement appeared in a local newspaper, I received a phone call from a woman executive at a large corporation. She was intrigued by the concept of outplacement but wanted to know why career counseling firms did not offer some kind of intervention service to help companies prevent those situations that make outplacement necessary.

Her point is well-taken, since most firings take place about 12 months after they should have. If problems could be identified beforehand, it would save a great deal of emotional investment on the part of both the company and the individual.

I've been convinced for many years that corporations would do well to offer their employees (certainly their management-level employees) a career reassessment program. It has been my privilege to work with a few companies that did — and with scores of individuals who did so privately and were better employees for it.

Such a reassessment would identify communications problems, help people reassess their careers, and help the company be more objective about the people who work for it.

Perhaps the two most crucial causes of employee unhappiness are the failure to openly communicate and the failure of the company to recognize that people change. After all, the position a person holds often doesn't change, while the person changes dramatically. The hole grows rounder while the peg grows squarer until an otherwise productive employee quits or is fired.

Of course, firings and resignations are a fact of business life, but one to be avoided. There is a measurable economic cost to a company when an employee of long standing must be replaced. One study placed it at $50,000 to $150,000 in lost efficiency and productivity.

If companies would help their people — make them feel like they're being listened to — they would see much greater loyalty, efficiency and productivity. As I've said many times before, people who feel that we've listened to them will give us anything we want. There is the risk, perhaps, that in helping employees reassess their careers, a company would lose some good people, but they would be rare exceptions. Moreover, losing an employee by a reasoned, mutual decision is far less traumatic to a company than having to fire someone who has become unhappy and unproductive.

Unfortunately, because our government pays unemployment benefits, it behooves the unhappy individual to get him or herself fired rather than to quit. I have worked with a number of people who either consciously or unconsciously activated all of the elements necessary to get themselves fired, often over a period of years, and at a great cost to their employers in terms of lost efficiency and productivity. Had someone been available to work with them before their problems got out of hand, a great deal of pain and trouble could have been saved on both sides.

> **The loss of a long-term employee,**
> **whether by firing or resignation,**
> **can have a real cost of $50,000 to $150,000**
> **in terms of lost experience and efficiency**
> **and the training of new personnel.**

Now, this being the real world, we must recognize that there are certain people who simply will never be good employees and some people who will never be good bosses. There are also some people who will simply never get along with each other, no matter what happens or who intervenes. But that does not absolve a corporation from its responsibility to encourage these people to be more than what they are.

Companies can — even without the help of a consultant — look for the signs of problems. They can see for themselves whether people still enjoy an easy camaraderie with their co-employees, whether they smile easily, whether they're decisive, or whether they're still capable of taking calculated risks. There may be issues not related to career that cause people to change, but without clear and open lines of communication, a company will never find out.

The ultimate fringe benefit a company can offer its employees is a graceful and beneficial way to leave. If the employee perceives that his or her continued employment with the company will be detrimental to personal career, then it will ultimately be good for both to pave the way.

I once asked the executive vice president of a major corporation how he would feel about offering some of his key executives the freedom to examine, and perhaps change, their careers. He said, "I'd be scared to death!" I told him he would certainly find that their loyalty would be even greater. I used an analogy which I believe is very apt: In the late 1980s, when the East Germans were told by their government that they could not leave, they left by the tens of thousands. When their government gave permission to leave, they turned around and went home.

The companies that help employees truly grow in their careers, rather than just providing them with jobs, will be so much the better for their efforts. The care and concern any business shows its employees is the fullest measure of its integrity and honesty. It has been my experience that such a firm will prosper.

———

It is not only humane, but it's also
the finest kind of public relations,
to extend real support and respect
to departing employees.

◆ Outplacement

According to one theory, the term "outplacement" originated in the early 1960s, when employment agencies and placement firms recognized a rich new market in working with just-fired or terminated employees and placing them in new positions as quickly as possible. The idea was that it is easier to place someone who has just been terminated than it is to place someone who has been unemployed for a period of time. In my experience, this is unquestionably true.

Since then, outplacement has come to encompass a much broader scope of services. In its fullest sense, outplacement includes working both with corporations in preparation for a firing or layoff, and with terminated employees, by way of a complete and comprehensive career guidance program. Some companies provide outplacement assistance through their own human resources department, but most engage the services of an outside consulting firm.

Avoidable Mistakes

Most employers find it very traumatic to fire an employee. It is an emotion-laden situation in which the employer and the employees's immediate manager genuinely feel badly about the necessity to take such a step. Concern for the individual who is being let go is intermixed with feelings of failure, sometimes anger against the employee, sometimes self-pity. The employer is therefore prone to make some rather serious mistakes because of the lack of objectivity in such a situation.

Invariably, because of this factor, most firings take place six to twelve months later than they should have, occasionally longer. When the problem is belatedly acknowledged, there is frequently an urgency to "get it over with" as quickly as possible. The resulting failure to plan, inadvertently causes unnecessary pain for the fired employee. For example, there have been far too many firings on wedding anniversaries, or on the birthday of the spouse or children of the employee, and other inappropriate occasions.

Companies should give serious thought to a truly beneficial severance program which can provide a "bridge" for the employee to his or her next position. Managers should fight against the very human tendency to hold a termination interview at 4:30 p.m. on a Friday so that they can have it over with, then go home and forget the entire ordeal. This, of course, leaves the terminated employee with an empty weekend to face family and friends with no access to professional help.

Benefits of Outplacement

An increasing number of companies are recognizing that it's in their economic and social self-interest to help terminated employees through what is, next to the death of a loved one, one of the most difficult crises they'll ever face.

A complete "outplacement" offering provides a "damage control" service in advance. It helps the employer soften his or her defensive posture, and in a positive sense, provides every possible assistance to the employee. It helps the manager who is to do the actual firing to plan and prepare what to say and what not to say during the termination interview. So often in the heat of the moment, such a person will unintentionally make statements which inspire lasting resentments and/or greatly weaken the employee's self-image.

It is best for everyone concerned that the consultant be present and meet with the employee immediately after the termination interview so that the employee can have the opportunity to vent the severe emotional trauma of the moment. When someone who is fired is given this opportunity, the negative emotions much more quickly run their course, and the individual can be helped to achieve an "onward and upward" frame of mind and begin making plans for the future.

In this fashion, a complete career guidance process can begin immediately. An employee will quickly overcome his or her resentment toward the company, and will be open to receive help in objectively reassessing his or her situation. An employee can quite quickly make a new decision as to whether to stay within the field of experience or move into a new one, and then learn the professional procedures required to penetrate the market in the chosen direction.

The initial half-hour or so with a newly terminated employee is particularly taxing and emotionally draining for a career consultant, but it has many rewards. Some individuals have asked me to accompany them home to help break the news to their families. I have accompanied fired personnel as they went to their desks to gather personal belongings — simply to provide moral support during a last half-hour in the company. When professional help is made available immediately, healing occurs quickly. If, however, the person is not given, or refuses, such help, the hurt and anger seems to solidify and becomes much more difficult to eradicate.

It is very common for individuals who have been terminated to speak of initiating lawsuits against the company. Spouses in their initial anger can encourage such action. But in all the outplacement cases I know in which individual attention was made immediately available, not one lawsuit has been initiated by a terminated employee against his or her former company. (My own recommendation is that a decision of that kind be postponed until a new career direction has been established. The energy, time and emotion expended on a lawsuit would be completely counterproductive for most people.)

There are other benefits to companies who provide outplacement support: Severance costs are reduced because employees generally find new jobs faster. In addition, the cost of such a service is saved many times over in good public relations alone. Morale among employees who remain with the company is improved, and furthermore, those who have been let go will generally acknowledge, "In spite of it all, they were very fair to me when it came time for me to leave."

The Company's Responsibility

Even though timely action in correcting a bad situation is imperative, a company must also consider what it owes a terminated employee. At the very least, it owes a recognition of what that employee has contributed and a recognition that the employee should be helped to retain a sense of self-worth.

If a company insists on reasonable understanding, care and concern for employees who are being terminated, that attitude more easily, perhaps automatically, suffuses and enhances employee relations and public image at every level. Certainly it can serve as the occasion to instill those attitudes.

The Role of the Outside Consultant

Now, what exactly does an outplacement consultant do? In a nutshell, he or she helps a company think through and prepare for every detail of the termination process. That could include thoroughly reviewing personnel policies, planning the termination methodology, and working out the details of the termination interview. In short, he or she strives to make the entire process as beneficial to both sides as possible.

Outplacement consultants generally come prepared with a complete checklist of items to be taken care of. It can include basics, such as doing the actual firing within the first five minutes of the termination interview, and specific details, such as checking personnel records to make sure the employee is not being fired on a birthday or anniversary. It can include detailed discussion of how best to deal with the variety of possible emotional reactions.

Company officials need to be aware that termination interviews are probably the single most mishandled business function there is. And the reason is simple lack of planning. Managers don't think about what they're going to say — and a person who is fired is going to remember every word for *years* afterward — so they hem and haw, or they're too severe, or they issue mindlessly insensitive platitudes.

After the interview, they don't know what to do with the terminated employee or how to allay the fears of the remaining employees. They're unprepared for the many different reactions they might get — shock, anger, denial, threats of violence — and their unpreparedness compounds a bad situation. The outplacement consultant helps them prepare.

Then the consultant works with the terminated employee(s), either to place them in a new position, learn more effective techniques for finding new positions, or to offer them career guidance. It's a win-win situation for all concerned.

Choosing the Right Consulting Firm

When you find yourself in the position of having to hire an outplacement consultant, there are a number of things to consider:

The firm's experience. How long have they been around and what is the background of the individual professional staff members? How many clients have they worked with over the years? Is outplacement a key part of their business or just a sidelight to the main part of their practice? What do their references, both corporate and individual, have to say about them?

While it's imperative to find good corporate references, I believe the real "proof of the pudding" is to be found in **the attitudes of terminated employees toward the outplacement firm.** Every career specialist worthy of the name has dealt with "informal" outplacement — individuals who were given no assistance by their company when they were fired, were badly battered in the following six to twelve months, and finally sought help using their own resources. The success the firm has had in helping such people cope with their resentment toward the company and their self-esteem problems, now solidified, provides clear evidence as to how well they will represent your corporation in outplacement services.

Breadth and Depth of Service

What is the scope of the services offered by the outplacement firm to the corporation? How much time will they actually spend with the company's management? Will they assure the confidentiality of their process — both toward your company and toward the ex-employee? And how will they do so?

What is their scope of services for the terminated employees? It could range from as little as a group seminar on resume writing to a high-quality placement program. Or it can be a very sophisticated, in-depth career guidance program providing reassessment, decision making, re-direction, and all-encompassing self-marketing processes.

In fact, outplacement firms will look pretty much the same on the surface, so it's important to visit each one you're considering in order to get a feel for them.

Look beyond the nice surroundings, the specialized equipment and services, e.g., videotaping, resume service, office, telephone (all of which can serve a real purpose), and determine the intensity of care, support and understanding provided to each individual at a much deeper level. It is this latter which ultimately redounds to your company's public image.

Effective Decision Making Support

Determine whether the firm is simply inclined to "place" people in something similar to their previous employment, or whether clients are helped toward a broader freedom of choice. If a firm offers both career guidance and placement services, even in ostensibly separate divisions, it is legitimate to question how much the listing of job opportunities may color the objectivity of the career guidance services.

What sort of guarantees do they offer? I don't know of any reputable firms that guarantee new jobs, but most will, at the very least, promise to work with the individual for an extended period of time, or better, until that person has been re-situated.

Cost is certainly a factor. Expect each firm to be clear and up front about its fee schedules. And of course, consider the personal chemistry. Make sure it's right.

Outplacement is a difficult and painful process. But with the services of a professional outplacement consultant, it can be smoother and easier — on both sides of the desk.

**The ultimate corporate benefit:
Helping employees attain
freedom of choice
in their personal career decisions.**

CHAPTER THIRTEEN

Case Histories

*I have learned that
suffering is neither good nor bad.
It's what you do with it that counts.*

— D. B., Client

In all cases cited in this book, names have been changed and descriptive detail altered to protect the privacy of each individual.

The cases have been carefully selected in order to illustrate the broad span of choice available to those who wish to make career changes, and to give practical examples of how a professional approach to personal career development will allow greater freedom for the individual in the marketplace.

◆ RECOGNIZING THE POSSIBILITIES

In the course of our lives we build walls around ourselves. We accumulate years of experience. We restrict our vision as to what our talents and experience permit us to envision for our lives. But if we can build such walls, then we can also tear those walls down, and open ourselves to possibilities which have never before crossed our field of vision.

Insurance Salesman Becomes Computer Service Marketing Executive

One of my earliest experiences as a career consultant was with Randy, who had spent all of his years in insurance sales. He had been a branch manager, making in 1990's terms, $40,000 to $50,000. He told me that his highest income had been $65,000 to $70,000 in a good year as a salesman.

In setting his career goals, Randy decided he would stay in the insurance industry, but move into the corporate and upper-management level. He had been at the branch and agency level for approximately 15 years.

During the career-guidance program, he came up with a list of industries he was considering for potential contacts. About fourth or fifth on his list was the computer industry. Another client asked him to explain why he had listed the computer field. He said, "I haven't the slightest idea. All I know about computers is that they do printouts."

His first contact in that field was a friend who was the president of what Randy believed to be a small computer company. He and this man had played golf every week, weather permitting, for about ten years, so they knew each other well, socially. To his great surprise, Randy discovered that his friend's company was larger than he had thought. It had branches throughout the United States and Europe.

He also discovered that his friend had a major problem: All of his management personnel were former computer technicians and not as capable at management and marketing as the president needed.

Randy had gone to his friend simply to get some referrals to insurance company presidents with whom he believed his friend was acquainted. He got the referrals, contacted the insurance company presidents, then went back to his friend to thank him for the leads.

During the second meeting, both began to realize that this company president had a marketing problem — on his shoulders was the whole load of administering the marketing program throughout the country and internationally — and his friend had years of experience in sales and marketing.

After about six weeks of on-again off-again negotiating, Randy accepted a position as international marketing director for that company. He more than doubled his income, and he proceeded, in about three years, to develop the marketing program of the company, increasing its gross revenue by 33 percent.

**In the course of our lives,
we build walls around ourselves ...
But if we can build such walls,
we can also tear those walls down.**

Dentist Starts New Life
In Completely Different Field

Among all the professionals I have worked with, Matthew, a dentist, was perhaps the most trapped in his field. All of the men in his family were dentists: His father was a dentist. His grandfather was a dentist. Most of his uncles and cousins were also in dentistry.

From childhood, Matthew assumed that his career would be in dentistry. He finished his schooling, then set up his practice.

After five years in a very successful practice, he became ill. His doctor told him that it was not a physical problem but rather something psychosomatic. After a second doctor agreed with the first, Matthew reluctantly agreed with the diagnosis.

He next concluded that the source of the problem must be his marriage. So he and his wife spent a good deal of time and money on marriage counseling. But the counselor suggested that, since their marriage seemed to be basically sound, the real cause of the problem must be something other than his marriage.

He slowly and reluctantly came to realize that he simply was uncomfortable in the practice of dentistry. This thought caused him to have major guilt feelings toward his family.

During the next year, he visited his alma mater for a class reunion, where he mentioned in a group meeting that he was thinking of leaving the practice of dentistry. He said the group, including one professor, vehemently urged him not to leave dentistry. The professor told him that he was one of the best students the school had ever turned out and he simply couldn't do that.

After another year or so in his practice, he finally sought help with his career. It was extremely difficult for him to leave dentistry. He so completely identified with the profession — from training, experience and family tradition — that he found it nearly impossible to recast his self-identity. It took months of reflecting and reading before he could finally achieve the freedom of mind to see himself as a person capable of doing just about anything he wanted.

When finally, in his own mind, he became a "non-dentist," it was a major relief for him. He did indeed leave the practice of dentistry. Eventually he became a successful property owner and developer.

Among other properties, he owned the building in which his dental practice had been located.

From Librarian to Operations Manager
To Business Owner

One day during her sophomore year in college, Barbara had a chance meeting in a corridor with one of her professors. She asked the professor for advice about her area of concentration.

The professor suggested that she pursue library science. She was, the professor said, one of the school's best statistical analysts. She should be good in library work, and it would provide a secure future.

Being impressionable, as most of us are at that age, Barbara dutifully majored in library science, got her degree, and then spent the next 20 years as a librarian.

When Barbara came to me, she was under intense stress. The major habit patterns she developed in library work (compiling, analyzing, filing) were in severe conflict with her personality. She was a strong "people-related" person who had spent two decades working primarily with books and systems. She should never have become a librarian. She was, in effect, a "walking conflict."

It took a good deal of re-thinking and reflecting for Barbara to rearrange her life, but she was able to accomplish it.

She was offered and accepted a management position with a family-run business. Her success in this role included skillful handling of some very delicate family relationships.

After a number of years, however, Barbara grew tired of the pressures on her from the family members. She left the company and founded her own financial advisory business.

◆ IF YOU THINK YOU CAN OR CAN'T ...
YOU'RE RIGHT.

Any effort to make a change in career patterns requires real courage and a willingness to make an act of faith in oneself. When it's done, however, the results are startling in terms of renewed self-confidence, hope and vigor, and a sense of well-being.

From Manufacturing, to Finance,
To Commercial Broadcasting

Eric and his wife, who lived in an eastern state, first came to my office during a summer vacation on the West Coast, where Eric grew up. At the time, he was general manager of a midsize manufacturing operation. He had a substantial salary but was quite unhappy because the owners, a family, never quite seemed to trust him, watching all his moves carefully. He could not be absent for any unexplained reasons without arousing suspicions in their minds.

He started our career-guidance program during his vacation. The following December, about the middle of the month, he called me to schedule an appointment during the week before Christmas. The season gave him the occasion to visit relatives on the West Coast and be absent from his job without arousing suspicion.

When he arrived, we had a long Friday afternoon session in which he explained to me that the situation at his company was becoming intolerable. As we talked, the conviction grew in him that he simply must take action. He called his wife.

During the phone conversation, they agreed that he should resign his position; they would move to the West Coast, and he would find a position after they arrived.

Compounding the difficulty in making this decision was the fact that they expected their first baby during the early part of January. They arrived between Christmas and New Year's.

After a series of productive interviews, and uncovering a number of different possibilities for himself, Eric accepted a good offer with a major brokerage house. He negotiated a higher-than-usual beginning salary. The firm sent him to New York City for training. He became one of the most productive stock brokers in his city.

Four or five years later, during a visit to my office, he revealed his most important goal. It had always seemed so farfetched that he had never discussed it before. For years he had had in the back of his mind the desire to own and operate a commercial radio station.

Now, he said, after years in the field of finance, he knew how to assemble the financing required for such a venture. He had formed a corporation. Two other people were involved with him in the venture, and he was leaving soon to go back to the East Coast to pursue his goal.

From Lab Technician
To Fashion Industry Professional

A health-care worker in her early 30s, Maria was torn by deep anxieties relating mostly to her parents. She had recently left home after a difficult disagreement with her mother and father.

She was raised in a strong religious atmosphere. As a result, she had an unconscious need to be obedient to her parents — which she vehemently denied — and had flown in the face of that. It was very difficult for her to come honestly to grips with those underlying pressures and to assume her own independent status.

After a year of on-again, off-again successes and failures, she wrote to me from another city. I didn't know she had left town. In her letter, she discussed her growing interest and involvement in the world of fashion:

"Since we last spoke, my life has been either a mountain of joy or a pit of despair; more of the joy than the despair. However, since your counseling I have been so much more alive, more and more self-assured, more confident and more positive in my involvement with people. So many times I have thanked myself for listening to that inner voice ... It's amazing how many people look at me blankly, not understanding, when I express to them my career change; the when, where, why and how of it all just leaves them amazed ...

"I have learned a lot about business in general since our last conversation, and I have plans to investigate the importing/exporting side of this industry. I have a very dear friend who has been involved in international business for a few years, and with time, I am learning bits and pieces of that business.

"I still want my own business and feel so confident and great about it. I have learned avenues of confidence in meeting potential business contacts and employers and confidence in being able to open and/or direct the course of conversation/communication. Thanks for bringing me to the realization that I can do it, it can be done, it will be done, and what I feared in the past is nothing but the past."

The Young Man Who Nearly Founded an Airline

Bill was an unusually impressive young man. He had had a good career in sales. He had made good money, but was also aware that he had not yet begun to tap his considerable talents.

In the course of his decision-making process, he developed what seemed to him an impossible dream. One of his major loves had always been airplanes. He decided to found an airline which would serve a very special purpose at a time (early 1970s) when there were long delays at most airline check-in counters for security reasons. He saw a need for a small feeder line which could avoid that particular inconvenience to passengers on shorter domestic flights.

Bill began to put together his plans. He made all the business contacts, did all the financial planning, and prepared all personnel and equipment plans which were required. Over a remarkably short time, he convinced the people who had to be convinced that he could do the job.

He obtained the loans which were required, found all the staff he needed — the pilots, flight attendants, technical personnel and others — and prepared manuals for training purposes.

He researched the kinds of equipment available — the type of planes which would be the most effective for the kind of flight distance involved, and the most cost effective in terms of the number of passengers which the airline could and would be expected to handle.

Bill ordered the planes that he wanted with modified engines suited to his purpose. He established contracts with businesses in several cities in the area he intended to service. In the course of a few months, Bill had developed a complete set of plans with the hundreds of details required to put together such an enterprise.

As the final steps were under way to initiate the airline, the gasoline shortage of the early '70s suddenly hit. Fuel was unavailable to him and he was forced to cancel the entire venture.

In spite of the disappointment, Bill told me that he had never before felt so good about himself nor so sure of his own abilities.

He knew that he had, in actual fact, founded an airline, and that it would have worked. That success gave him the courage to strive toward more demanding responsibilities. In his next step, he became a vice president in a large marketing organization.

A Whole New Field: Agricultural Equipment

Cliff, a young man in his late 20s, chose the field of agricultural equipment, fully aware that sales in the industry were low during the recession of 1981-82.

He began making contacts with agricultural equipment companies. Two or three weeks later, he called to say he had an important appointment that afternoon with an agricultural equipment firm and needed help to control his anxiety.

Cliff had a specific offer from the president of the company, contingent on the concurrence of the firm's marketing director. He was scheduled to meet that afternoon with both men. He had two additional offers from other companies, but preferred this particular company and position.

In order to help him achieve the right frame of mind for the interview, I simply had to ask two questions. The first was: "Have you ever met the marketing director?" His answer was, "No". The second question was: "What will you do if you decide you don't like the marketing director and that you couldn't work with him?" His answer to that was, "I wouldn't take the job even if it was offered to me."

All he had to hear then was, "Why don't you simply go over and find out if you want to work with the marketing director?"

He went to the interview, was offered the job, and he accepted it.

"I have met the enemy and he is me."

Financial Company President "Paints His House"

There is severe emotional pressure when a person loses a position and is faced with the need of finding another source of income. Sam's is a special case.

Five years earlier, Sam had accepted the position as president and CEO of a company without realizing that it was on the verge of bankruptcy. Having signed the contract, however, he proceeded to make the necessary contacts, establish the kind of confidence with financial institutions required to float the necessary loans, and almost single-handedly pulled the company back from the brink.

One year later, the company was not entirely healthy, but it was quite clearly safe. At the annual meeting of the stockholders and board of directors he was praised by the group because he had saved their investment.

He continued to build the company. After a total of five years, he had quintupled its revenue and net worth, and had made many positive contributions to the life of the company.

At that point, with the company in good health, the principal stockholder of the company fired him. This was a major blow to Sam — the company he had saved was now taken from him. But he had no alternative, so he started to rethink and reshape his career.

When we came to the point in our career guidance program when interviews should begin, he refused. His style, he said, was to hear the entire package first. When the formal sessions were completed, he assured us he would start his interview program immediately.

Suspecting he would have a problem, I called him the next week. He told me he had just realized that in five-years' time, because of the pressures of his position, he had done no work around his house and felt he owed it to his wife to do so.

He said, "I'm painting the living room now. I'll start my interview program when it's finished."

The following week when I asked him if he had started, he said, "I had the equipment out, so I thought I'd also paint the kitchen. I'll start when that's completed."

The next week he was painting the dining room, the week after that he was painting a bedroom, and the following week another bedroom. So I asked him to come see me.

I told him that he needed to face the fact that he was frightened and if he did not face it, he would never solve his career problem. He became angry with me because, after all, top executives are never frightened.

After a good deal of insistence on my part, he finally relaxed and told me that I was right — he was afraid that he would not be able to return to the level of his previous job. What bothered him most was the thought that some company president, during an interview, would feel sorry for him. He said, "I couldn't take that."

He had his first interview the next day. Having faced the fact that he was afraid, he then overcame that fear and acted in spite of it. Prior to that, he denied the existence of the fear. It therefore controlled him — it caused him to paint his house, convincing himself and everyone else that he was not afraid.

These kinds of emotions are part and parcel of every career move. If you do not deal honestly with them, your emotions will control and curtail productive activity, thereby reducing your freedom of action. On the other hand, if you honestly acknowledge the presence of these emotions and the impact they are having, you will be able to control them and make effective career moves.

Within three months, Sam accepted the presidency of a company in another state.

Strongest Negative Reaction to
The Concept of Power

For more than 20 years, I have asked each of my clients at an appropriate point in the career guidance program, "Do you like power?" The purpose was to determine whether some hidden negative attitude towards the possession and exercise of authority adversely affected the individual's career. Over the years, I received three general responses: From modest denial to emphatic denial to a pre-definition before giving an answer.

Ralph's response was so violently negative that I never again asked the question. When I asked, "Do you like power," he became angry and red in the face and his hands began to tremble. He told me in a strained voice that I had no right to ask such a question and asked what I meant by it. If I meant power over life and death, he said, slamming his fist on my desk, of course he would not want it. If I meant to have the power to control people's lives (slamming his fist on my desk again), he certainly wouldn't want it. He delivered a lecture regarding military generals and the kind of mentality that could send people to their deaths. He gave perhaps four or five definitions of power, denying emphatically in each case that he would be interested.

His career had been a disaster. He simply allowed himself, in a passive way, to be at the beck and call of his bosses and simply "do what had to be done." His attitude made it impossible for him to aspire toward any kind of responsibility and authority. He refused most of the promotions he had been offered during his career.

Sadly, this is one of the very few clients who, in my view, did not achieve a notable success. While he did effectively negotiate better salaries and was quite content with new-found responsibilities, he did not effectively use the considerable talents he had.

Determining a valid career goal is usually difficult. Some-times there can be some major mental blocks which keep us from acknowledging what we really want to do. The following case is an example of a difficult mental block:

Navy Officer Returns to His First Love

After ten years in the Navy and an early promotion, Albert, age 32, had a very difficult year which prompted him to resign his commission. He had intended to stay in the Navy. Now his career was in a shambles.

He floundered for a year or more. He took some temporary positions, but was unable to find a good means of income.

After starting to plan his career, he found it very difficult to make a decision. His first choice was to get into some phase of electronics, since he had been well trained in that field during his naval career. After pursuing a number of contacts along that line, however, he lost interest.

He repeated the decision-making process. This time he chose hobby shops. He thought perhaps some day, he would open a store which would sell hobby items to hobbyists and also train people in hobbies they might be interested in pursuing.

He began making some excellent contacts with some of the major stores in his city, but did not take a position. It seemed to me he had not identified what he really wanted. We spent a great deal of time discussing his decision and the potential mental blocks which might be holding him back.

One day, exuberated, he came to me with his decision made. He finally had realized that he had gone into the Navy not because he was particularly patriotic, nor drawn to military life, but simply because he loved ships and the sea. The traumatic experience he had in his last year with the Navy had developed a mental block which temporarily hid from him what he was truly interested in.

A few weeks after that realization, he accepted a position as shipmaster in a very large company which provided dry-dock facilities for ocean-going vessels.

His position gave him responsibility for 300 to 1,500 personnel, depending upon the size of the ship in dry dock for repair. He loved his work. The company gave him good upward mobility. Later he was offered the position of manager of an overseas port.

In the following years, and through several restructurings, he continued with the company. Many years later, he was part of a small team to remain with the company during dissolution proceedings.

His most recent career move was toward recreational boats and boating.

**Any effort to
make a change in career patterns
requires real courage
and a willingness
to make an act faith in oneself.**

♦ MAKING MAJOR CHANGE

None of us should be slotted according to background or train-
ing or experience, either in our minds or in the minds of others.
If we are to avoid this slotting, then we must individually take the
initiative to expand our horizons.

Oil Company Executive
Becomes University Professor

One of the really remarkable career moves is the one made by Gordon, an oil company executive, in the early 1970s. In today's dollars, his salary was in the $250,000 to $300,000 range.

He was disillusioned by what for him was inappropriate activity by the oil companies in the world market. He voluntarily left his position with the intention to simply find another executive position in another industry — just so it wasn't oil.

After an initial reassessment of his options and a review of the market, Gordon began to recall an interest he had during his high school years to become a university professor. But circumstances at the time took him in another direction.

He felt the idea was impractical, and he was embarrassed even to bring it up, both because of his age (55) and because he had only a bachelor's degree with no graduate studies. After discussion, however, he agreed to keep the idea in mind and to talk it over with his wife.

After a three to four week soul-searching process, he and his wife decided he should take the time to investigate the possibility.

He did a remarkable job of negotiating. Three Eastern universities offered him the opportunity to teach, with the understanding that, at his own pace, he would pursue higher studies. He accepted one of the positions beginning that fall term, called me the following March — he was preparing his taxes — to tell me that he and his wife were happier than they had ever been before.

Gordon and his wife had not realized how much they disliked the social and political pressure of the corporate setting. They had changed their life-style to their own liking. Moreover, he said, they were saving more money than ever before on a fraction of his former income. The reduction in social expenditures, the less pretentious life style, and a different tax bracket all combined to have them in a better financial position.

The change for both Gordon and his wife was a major one — perhaps more difficult than a culture change. It required for both of them a difficult internal adjustment to an entirely different way of life. The result was complete contentment with a new and revised career and life setting.

From Teaching to Travel Agency

Having taught for more than 13 years, including posts in overseas locations, Cathy decided finally that she wanted to leave the field of education completely. She thought she might capitalize on her travels and her experience in cross-cultural living.

She decided to pursue a career in some aspect of international travel.

She started with a travel agency. The pay was not very high, but at the same time she justified the move on the basis of the travel that she and her husband could undertake at reduced cost both with airlines and with hotels. In addition to that, it seemed to be a necessary step for her to move in the direction that she really wanted to go.

She visited me several times in the next few years. The work was enjoyable, and the benefits of inexpensive travel and lodging allowed her and her husband to travel extensively. But the pay was not at all satisfactory. However, each time her dissatisfaction crescendoed, she received a promotion — temporarily resolving the problem.

After three years, she was appointed a vice-president of the firm, with a substantial raise in salary and the opportunity to become a partner. She had reached her goal.

From Hard Goods to Fish Flour

Dave, who had been involved in hard-goods manufacturing and sales, decided that he wanted to build his career in the fish flour industry. (Fish flour is produced by drying dead, even rotting fish and reducing them to a fine powder which looks like flour. The resulting high-protein product, which has been prepared and distributed in underdeveloped countries, has a great deal of importance in areas of the world where starvation is prevalent.)

Dave began talking to people in the fishing industry who would have knowledge of this particular product. One of the people he talked to was the president of a company in Seattle with several subsidiary companies, each relating to a different aspect of the fishing industry, and who had invested heavily in the production of fish flour.

**When people examine their careers
with an open mind,
they invariably make significant changes.**

On his first visit to this man, Dave was well received but, as he told me later, was given to understand that there were no positions available; the president left such matters to the heads of his subordinate companies.

I encouraged Dave to make a second visit because the company president was acquainted with the fishing industry not only on the West Coast of the United States, but throughout the world as well. Such a person would be a good contact for the future development of Dave's career.

When Dave called the company president to arrange another appointment, however, he found the man to be quite reluctant to see him, insisting that it should be enough to talk for a few minutes by telephone. As a seasoned salesman, however, Dave continued to press for a personal meeting. After some minutes during which he kept repeating this idea, the company president suddenly capitulated and asked him if he would be free to come in the next morning at 10:00.

During the meeting, Dave asked the company president why he suddenly had agreed to see him after his initial reluctance. The president was somewhat embarrassed and said that there was something that this young man as a newcomer to the fish flour industry wouldn't know: On the assumption that there is a lot of money in the product, some people would like to make a temporary entry into the fish flour industry, make a good profit and then get out. He told Dave that he was the first person he had talked to who was honestly and sincerely interested in the field. He simply had to be sure.

The president then referred Dave to the president of a subsidiary company who was looking for a marketing director.

Vice President in Clothing Establishment To Account Executive, Computer Services

Rod selected the computer field as his target. He had a good deal of business experience (retail clothing), but he had no formal training in the computer field. This was the mid-1970s, when it was considered impossible to make any headway in the computer field without extensive technical training. A number of people he contacted initially told him that his goal was impractical.

He was able to overcome these obstacles. It was clear that he had exceptional talent for management, and that he was adept at, and very sensitive to, customer relations.

The computer services company which hired him had an account amounting to several million dollars per year in fees. One of the technicians of the consulting company was in charge of the work, but the client company was very unhappy with the service.

Rod was assigned to the account, and, using his human relations and management skills, quickly ascertained the nature of the customer's complaints, and resolved the difficulties. Rod was recognized as being directly responsible for saving a multi-million dollar source of revenue. Fifteen years later, still with the company, he is a recognized expert in specialized commercial computer applications.

Professional people — doctors, lawyers, dentists, teachers, clergymen, etc. — as a rule have a harder time making a transition from their careers into a new field. The reason seems to be that there is a greater amount of ego involvement for such people with their profession; there has been a great deal of time, money and energy expended in acquiring the credentials to operate within the profession, and as a result, there is also a fear that this specialization has made it next to impossible for the individual to do anything else. Moving beyond this fear is, indeed, possible.

Physician Who Modified His Practice

Physicians as a group have the most difficult time in developing the frame of mind required to freely leave their field. The following case, however, was an exception.

Doctor George was a specialist. He worked for a major hospital conglomerate, and by any standards, he made a great deal of money. He found the closed ranks of the medical world, particularly as it exists around hospitals, and the elevated stature given to and/or assumed by doctors to be distasteful.

Therefore he wanted to make some changes in his life and somehow continue on in the medical world.

He developed an entirely different kind of practice in which he provided temporary support to physicians in private practice. He spent about a third of each year in different parts of the country giving that kind of support. He also began to develop some farm land for purposes of raising and marketing exotic plants for use in the production of pharmaceutical drugs.

It seems to be generally true that people who have made a study of psychology and counseling will have assessed themselves more completely and honestly than most other people. Counselors are usually aware that they have this deeper self-knowledge, but they may be unaware that a good career decision requires still more self-examination.

It is easy for any of us who are knowledgeable in a field to simply apply ourselves to and identify ourselves with that field without ever taking an occasion to step back and dispassionately view our own objective relationship to it.

Doctor of Psychology

The first psychologist with whom I worked — let's call him Arnold — had been the head of the department of psychology in an Eastern college. The conviction had been growing in him that education, psychology, and counseling were not appropriate careers for him. After several years of painful soul searching, he left his post and began to think of new career directions.

As he began the process of career reassessment, Arnold tended to be somewhat defensive. He made it clear that whatever I suggested he re-think was something he had already come to terms with many years earlier. I had to insist that he was being defensive and that he make an intensive effort to question many of his attitudes and assumptions.

After several days of mulling over some reading material I had suggested for him, he told me with some astonishment that the reading material had allowed him, for the first time in his life, to "really apply my own psychology to myself."

Arnold's first step was to leave direct counseling and teaching and take over the management of a large counseling/consulting organization.

Doctor of Psychology II

John had operated his own counseling clinic for nearly 20 years before deciding to leave the field and carve out a new career for himself. He seemed considerably more open than the other psychologist I just mentioned, although there were overtones of the same problem.

I suggested the same reading material to him, and, after about a week, he called me and said that the books had made him very angry. The emotion was so unwarranted that he forced himself to sit back and ask himself why he had such a reaction.

He began to realize that he was jealous of an author who had been able to write quite simply and clearly about psychology in a popular style and whose books were selling well. (He himself had written an unsuccessful book.)

After he had come to grips with this reaction, he was able then to turn back to the material once more and deal with it more honestly. Like the other man, he said that he was able to identify in himself attitudes and assumptions which he had never before clearly dealt with.

He became a university professor.

♦ CAREER CHANGE WITHIN THE SAME
   ## COMPANY OR FIELD

It is a matter of experience that when people examine their careers with an open mind, they will decide to make significant changes. About 80 percent of people I have worked with have changed fields. But 20 percent have stayed in their original field of training and experience and nevertheless have made significant changes. A few have repositioned themselves in the same company. The following cases are examples of how this might be:

From Secretary to Operations Manager
To Leading Salesperson at a Brokerage Firm

Stella, a client during the late 1970s, had risen from secretary to branch operations manager in a brokerage firm in a period of 12 years.

She then felt "dead-ended" and thought it necessary to leave the field because she had no place to move within her own company. Advancement in the field would require a move to a headquarters company in New York City, which she was unwilling to do.

After exploring other options, she decided to stay in the field and to stay in the same company. But she negotiated a change which to this day is considered to be impossible: She moved from the operations side of the company to the sales side. Although she had never envisioned herself in sales, she began to realize she had the ability to sell. After another 10 years (a total of 20 plus years) with that company, she became one of its two consistent top producers.

In one sense, she made no career change, since she remained in the same company. But in another sense, she made a dramatic change in assuming entirely different responsibilities.

Director of State-Wide Press Association
Becomes Director of Larger Press Association

John had been director of the press association in a major Western state. He sought help because he felt that he could improve his situation. Since he was not permitted the kind of budget required to do an adequate job, he believed that it was only sensible for him to think of moving and changing to a different field.

In the course of his reassessment, he found that the press association of a major Eastern state was looking for a new director. To broaden his range of alternatives, he applied for that position. He was later chosen as one of the finalists and was asked to appear before the board of that press association for an interview.

We then scheduled a number of coaching sessions so he could prepare for that kind of interview. (The group interview poses special kinds of challenges.)

He handled the interview expertly. Afterwards, he returned to his hotel, packed and left for the airport to return home.

While at the airport, he met his predecessor, the director of the press association, who asked him, "Where have you been? The board has been trying to reach you; they want to offer you the job." He had no way of contacting the association from the airport, so he simply boarded the plane and flew home where he found three messages from the board chairman awaiting him.

He returned the call and negotiated a salary increase of $6,000.

Dairy Company President Becomes Regional Manager For a National Dairy Products Company

Nearly 20 years ago, Bill came to me in a deeply depressed and remorseful, nearly suicidal, state. Just a week or so earlier during a stockholders' meeting, he had voted his own stock to have himself removed as president of the company he had founded.

He owned approximately 35 percent of the company and the remaining shares in the company were distributed among seven or eight additional stockholders; none of them individually had a great deal of power.

When the motion was made that he should step down as president, the only way that it could carry was for him to vote his own shares against himself. Because of the arguments that were standard in that group, he told me it was in a burst of anger that he determined to vote against himself.

The next day, after his anger subsided, he bitterly regretted his action because he was left without income. His shares in the company could not be converted to cash and he had put most of his money into the company. The only way that he and his family could survive was for him to use a trust fund which had been established for his 20-year-old daughter who insisted that he take the money.

In the next few days, he heard that a national dairy products company was looking for a district manager in the Northwest. Bill decided that he simply had to have that job. We gave him a crash course in interview techniques which included methods of negotiation and some of the difficult questions that can occur in interviews.

He then attended the dairy association convention of his state. He had been a past officer of the organization and therefore knew his way around. Having arrived at the convention, he arranged to be introduced to the vice president representing the national dairy products company, and, having met the man, arranged to have lunch with him the following day.

At the luncheon he found three people at the table — the vice president and two assistants. They all were rather grim; this was, after all, an *interview* and they were going to examine this man very critically.

After lunch when they had settled back for coffee, the vice president began to ask questions. Bill told me later that one of the first questions was, "How did you get into your field?" and Bill replied, "Because I have warm hands."

Everyone laughed at the dairy industry humor. This light touch gave Bill a strong position during the meeting.

In a subsequent meeting, the vice president asked Bill how much of a salary he expected. In good negotiating posture, Bill said he would leave that to the vice president since he had no idea what the salary levels were in the company.

In the final analysis, Bill negotiated $5,500 above the first offer, and a raise of another $5,000 within the first 60 days.

Bill started immediately as a district manager in the Northwest, and then within six months, was promoted to a larger district in the Midwest. After his self-induced career crash, Bill went from despondency to a good job, to a raise, to a promotion — all within six months.

From Failure ... to Success as a Teacher

Don had been hurt so badly that he felt he had no recourse except to leave teaching and education entirely. As a matter of fact, he did leave for a short period of time and then went back into teaching. Following is an excerpt from his letter written about two years later:

"I just happened to think of you and all the help you gave me, so I wanted you to know what I am doing. I returned to teaching in September at the new school, teaching English. I am very happy and thankful for God's blessings. I can't thank you enough for your kindness, understanding and career and personal advice.

"I came to you with full trust in your abilities. I was a broken individual with a low self-esteem. You gave me courage and a feeling of importance and worth. I had the chance to explore areas of publication, but nothing worked out. I returned to substitute teaching a year ago in September after a year of a disappointing landscaping business. The substituting was originally for financial reasons, but I found out I enjoyed it and that there were good schools and good administrators, following my disappointments ...

"Since I have a master's degree in secondary ed. and English and 45 additional hours, I fit at the top of the salary schedule. Thus, getting another training position wasn't easy. But the new school offered me my full teaching experience and salary of $XX, plus good benefits. That's good for a teaching salary. We moved in August, and I really like my new job. I am teaching advanced writing, contemporary composition, and introduction to literature. The kids are wholesome, so I have very few discipline problems. Because of my tremendous personal and spiritual growth, I am a much better teacher than ever before. I am more understanding and thankful. I feel good about myself and the use of my talents. And now I am able to help others face the same problems I had. I have learned that suffering is neither good nor bad. It's what you do with it that counts.

"Because my life is richer, I will be happier in all things. ...all the things I wanted in a job I now have — creativity, independence, management, control of my teaching, support from positive, professional co-workers, and a good working environment in a three-year-old school, and an academic challenge".

It is a magnificent experience to see people who are beaten almost to despair take charge of events and turn their lives around.

◆ OVERCOMING PERCEIVED OBSTACLES
TO SUCCESS

Remember, factors that you or others may be accustomed to believing are disadvantages to career advancement — ranging from age, race, or religion, to highly specialized background, to education level — can be overcome by a careful, professional presentation of yourself.

High Ranking Military Officer
Becomes Low-Cost Housing Director

Ken was 55 years old when he and I began working together. His was a classic success in terms of career change.

He was born on the East Coast. He grew up in the military, spent most of his life in the military, rose to the rank of colonel, retired, and then settled in the West.

He had exceptional experience in the armed services. He had risen to the highest responsibility given to his rank. He was a veteran of the second world war and of many other campaigns. He had his own private assurance of being promoted to general if he remained in the service. But he decided to retire while he was still young enough to have a good career in civilian life.

After he completed the career guidance program, unlike most of my clients, he applied for an advertised position — the directorship of a private low-cost housing program, which received funding from every level of government. Since the job description clearly specified the experience the candidates were expected to have, Ken knew that the standard materials (resumes and other historical documentation) would undoubtedly rule him out on the basis of paperwork alone. So he developed materials which were completely accurate and truthful in describing his considerable responsibilities, but which did not disclose that, for 30 years, he had been a military officer.

He survived the first cut and was among the remaining 100 applicants — out of nearly 400 — who were contacted by telephone. He was asked where he had done the things described in his application materials. With the unusual self-assurance and gra-ciousness he possessed, he declined to tell the caller, simply giving assurance that he would, at the appropriate time with the board of directors, explain that experience in detail. In the meantime, he assured the caller, what he had done was exactly the kind of experience that the organization's job description called for.

He was then chosen to be among 30 finalists who would be required to visit the headquarters and talk to one of the personnel department staff. In the course of that interview, he was again asked to disclose more precisely the nature of the experience that he had had. He again smilingly refused, explaining again that he felt it would be better if he disclosed that information directly to the board of directors when the time came for that meeting.

He then made the next reduction down to ten. These ten final-ists were to engage in a series of interviews with their future subordinates — department heads and other supervisors.

By this time a good deal of curiosity had been aroused about him. While Ken was waiting in the reception area for one of those interviews, the chairman of the board walked by, introduced him-self, and asked Ken who he was. Ken gave his name, and the chairman said, "You're the man whose resume doesn't really tell us anything."

The point, of course, is that the resume among several hun-dred *did* gain the attention of the chairman of the board.

Ken handled that with his usual easy confidence. He cour-teously told the chairman of the board that he disagreed: Every point on his resume accurately matched the kind of experience and responsibility the job description required. The chairman was in no position to pursue the matter further at that time.

Ken then became one of three finalists. Each was to have two final meetings, one with the search committee which had initiated the process of recruiting the new director, and the final meeting with the 15 member board of directors.

The search committee again asked for details of Ken's ex-perience, but he again graciously but firmly suggested that, since the committee members were all board members, he would prefer to wait for the meeting of the full board to disclose those details.

At the board meeting the next day, the curiosity level was high. A member of the board began to question Ken closely about his experience, systematically leading to a disclosure of the location, the organization and the position in which Ken had had those experiences.

The board's attention, in an atmosphere in which one could hear a pin drop, was fixed on the conversation.

When Ken gave the name of the well-known military installation where he was last stationed, the questioner asked him, "Were you a civilian employee of the armed services?" Ken said "No, I was a member of the armed services." The interviewer then asked, "What rank were you?" Ken responded "I was a full colonel." At this point there was something of a sigh in the room — the board members had their curiosity satisfied.

While everyone was digesting this information, Ken passed around a carefully prepared qualifications summary and other materials, explaining precisely what he had done. His duties were such that in effect he managed a very large city. He was responsible for the transportation of hundreds of thousands of troops; he was responsible for the building and tearing down of housing units; supplied foodstuffs and clothing for military personnel and their families, was responsible for the equipment required for the efficient functioning of a very large military base.

It became very clear to the board as he talked that what he had done was directly pertinent to what they were trying to do. He was hired for the position even though the other two finalists had extensive experience in similar organizations.

Ken told me later that he knew, without doubt, that if even one step earlier he had revealed that he had been in the military, the word would have spread. There would have been a bias develop against him, a mindset that would have ruled him out of consideration for the position.

College Vice President
Becomes Law Firm Administrator

The decision about a new career goal after 20 years in university administration was very difficult for Susan. As a matter of fact, she made a number of wrong turns. She spent some time in the financial world on a commission basis, which was disastrous for her. Her self-image problem became distinctly worse.

One of Susan's initial concerns was that the business world would lose interest in her when it learned that she had been in education most of her career life.

She later told me that she had four successful interviews before she was finally asked by one of the interviewers, "By the way, what have you been doing?" to which she replied, "I have been in management for years — I'm a vice president." The person she was talking to simply said, "Oh." (Properly approached, employers are not necessarily intent on examining a person's job history.)

As time went on, Susan began to realize how much control she could exercise over her own career activities. She became much more comfortable in the interview setting and developed a very large list of new contacts.

She spent some time in the medical field and held a major administrative post for a number of years. She went on to decide that she would make another change: She began to approach law firms.

One day during lunch with a senior partner of a law firm, the lawyer mentioned that his firm was becoming large enough that it was time they hired an administrator. That conversation developed into a direct offer — Susan became the administrator of that firm. Later she joined another law firm in the same capacity.

Corporate Engineer, to City Engineer
To Engineering Company President

Fred, an engineer, left his company when it cut back severely. He became city engineer in a major city on the West Coast. His annual budget was 50 to 60 million dollars. He was responsible for a number of different bureaus and several thousand people.

For a year he loved the job. He told me that in many ways it was far more challenging and rewarding than any work he had previously had. The pay was far better than that of his previous job, and there were important fringe benefits, including the social life which both he and his wife enjoyed, and a city limousine at his personal disposal.

He called me one day, however, to say that some clouds were beginning to form. Whenever he took a problem to the city council, its members did not really concentrate on the problem, but rather postured for the media. They were politicians. He said, "While I always thought I understood the nature of politics, I didn't fully realize how much it would bother me to work with politicians."

Fred continued as city engineer for another four years. At the end of that time, having finally acknowledged the full extent of his discontent, he resigned. Therefore, he had to re-design his career, and he contacted me to help him.

Fred was one of those many people for whom *intrinsic reward* is terribly important: Personal pride and satisfaction in work.

When he re-thought his career after the five-year job as city engineer, the evidence was that he was now focused on *extrinsic reward*: Factors such as money and recognition. To justify staying in a position whose political nature was abhorrent to him, he concentrated on the *extrinsic* factors of unusually good salary, social life, city limousine, public recognition — to name a few.

After four years of forcing himself to stay in the uncomfortable setting, he developed the habit of looking to the extrinsics. So he was in danger of moving into another position which he might have chosen almost solely because of the good salary and other extrinsic considerations.

When Fred understood the effect his previous experience had upon him, he turned back to management and engineering as his real areas of expertise and knowledge. He determined that he was capable of executive-level responsibilities, approached an engineering firm in another state and was hired as president of that company. He has continued his career along similar lines ever since.

Age Is No Obstacle

My two oldest clients were 63 when they started our program. The first one, William, had been the manager of an advertising agency and was in the process of closing down the firm on behalf of the owner, who was his friend. Very anxious and upset, he started the career-guidance progam.

He made a complete transition, quickly moved into commercial real estate, and joined a fairly prominent firm. Within two months, he sold property which that firm had been trying to sell for more than four years. He told me later that his first commission check was in excess of $120,000 (in 1993 dollars) and that he had never in his life had so much money handed to him.

As he became more knowledgeable about his new field, he realized that he needed a firm with a different management style. About six months later, he changed to another, more prominent firm.

About 12 years later, when he was 75 years old, we received a note from him telling us that all had gone well and he was now semi-retired.

Age Is No Obstacle II

Ronald, another 63-year-old client, made a complete career change, but in his original field.

When we first saw him, Ronald appeared very old — perhaps in his mid- to late 80s. He had little energy, and he was nearing hopelessness, brought on by recent tragic events, coupled with his realization that he had no retirement income.

A widower, he had married his best friend's widow during the past year. But it turned out that this relationship was unsatisfactory: His new wife was a very successful career woman, but he had lost his position in his company of many years, and her continued success made his own lack of success even harder to bear.

After he spent some time reassessing his situation and making some firm decisions about his future, he began to regain his lost vigor. Someone on our staff remarked that he was behaving as if he were once again 40 years old.

For the first time in his life, he became a company president; it was a large company whose sales territory extended from Chicago to Europe. He managed the company successfully and finally retired in his early 70s.

Youth Is No Obstacle

Patricia was about a year out of high school when, with the support of her parents, she undertook the career guidance program. A painfully shy person, she had a very difficult time meeting people and found it impossible to envision herself in a successful career role.

About six months later, Patricia had apparently overcome her shyness and had become remarkably self-confident. Her mother called and related how Patricia had just returned from an interview in which the employer had been quite rude and discourteous. She said her daughter came home, told her parents about the incident, suggested that the man must have problems, and then cheerfully went to her room and turned on her sound system.

Her mother said that a year earlier, her daughter would have cowered in her own room for a couple of weeks before recovering from that kind of incident.

Not long after, Patricia moved away from home, to another city, and took a challenging job at a resort.

**Factors which we are led to believe
are obstacles to our career development —
such as age, religion, education, race, gender —
are readily overcome by a professional approach.**

♦ RECOGNIZING EARLY LIFE PATTERNS

Attitudes and values acquired in early life can become so ingrained in us that they can be difficult to clearly understand or to cope with in later life if they do not fit the changes in our lives or surroundings. They can constitute an "ego foundation" which can be so much a part of us as to reduce our freedom of choice. When we consciously focus on them, we can consciously oppose them or freely accept them. Take a look at the following examples:

Making No More Than Enough to Live On

Andrew came from what he described as a fundamentalist up-bringing. His religious training as a boy was very strict. As a young adult, he had dropped all pretense of religion and become an agnostic. All he wanted, he repeated again and again, was to make a lot of money.

At a later session with his wife present, he said it once again. I said, "I don't believe that — you're protesting too much." He was very upset that I questioned his motives. So I asked his wife what she thought. She said, "He doesn't mean it. I've heard him say that for years and I know it's not true."

This sparked a heated discussion between them. In the course of the argument, he suddenly became silent, lost in thought. Finally, he said, "I just remembered something I haven't thought of in years. When I was a boy, my father told me over and over, 'You should never want to make more on a job than just enough to live on — anything more than that is sinful.' I never wanted to believe that, but I believe I have been unconsciously obeying my father all my life." He had never made more than just enough to live on.

His father's admonition had created in him a need not to succeed. With this new insight, he finally overcame the problem and achieved his first real success.

A Clergyman Who Moved to Diet Counseling, Then Manufacturing

Robert had been a pastor in his church for many years. An activist in the 1960s, he later became bored with the routine of local church activities. He left the active ministry in his mid-40s and, somewhat predictably, moved into a job which was related to what he had been doing: He became a counselor in a diet program.

Since it had become second nature for him to motivate and counsel, it was easy for him to encourage overweight people to stay on a prescribed diet. Because Robert was a very strong person, however, it didn't take long before he and the owner of the firm were at odds. When the relationship became particularly disagreeable, he sought help in redesigning his career.

Most of his first thoughts took him toward service concepts, particularly counseling. He was in the process of divesting himself of conditioning from a life devoted, since childhood, to serving others.

After a good deal of in-depth re-thinking and mulling over the possibilities in the market, he joined another man as a partner in a manufacturing enterprise. This lasted no more than a year or two when, again, his personality clashed with his partner. This time, however, he acquired full ownership of the manufacturing firm.

After a few months in managing his own company, he told me, with surprise in his voice, that for the first time in his life he was simply and happily concerned with taking care of himself and his family. He no longer had to have the broader purpose of service to all humankind.

He felt as if a burden had been lifted from his shoulders.

The Inherited Business

At the age of 50, Gary was in the process of selling his well-known family business. During the past few years he had come to realize that he was burned out with the work and had never been very happy with it. He had been associated with it since he was a boy. As a young man, Gary never questioned whether he should take over the business or not. It was simply understood that he would do so at the proper time.

His initial intention was simply to seek a high level position in some existing business, working as an employee. But over the years, he had become very independent and self-sufficient. He began to realize that he could never comfortably work for anyone else. He therefore simply started another business in an entirely different field.

This time, since the business was in an industry he had personally chosen, he found it exciting and satisfying. Before, he said, he always had the spectre of family traditions within which he felt bound to operate.

> **Years of experience and conditioning can establish patterns in our minds which limit our vision and, therefore, our freedom of choice.**

Not only can early life experiences limit freedom in career choice, but beyond that, they can implant a need to fail, or at least a need not to succeed. The following cases exemplify the negative effects of such experiences on self-image and consequently on career success:

From Bookkeeper to Self-Employed

In 15 years, Michael had never risen above relatively low supervisory roles, and he made barely enough to support his family. He worked as a bookkeeper for years. When he decided to reassess his career, he was selling cemetery lots and doing poorly.

Because of his obvious competence, he had been offered many promotions, but he refused all of those which would put him into positions of real authority. In addition, three times when he knew he was being considered for a promotion, he unconsciously made mistakes which would result in his being taken out of consideration.

It was clear that he had a major conflict in relating to authority and authority figures. It was necessary that he understand the conflict and resolve it.

After a week or so of reading and reflection, he drew his own conclusion. For the first time in his life, he acknowledged that he harbored a deep resentment toward his father for physical punishment routinely and almost daily inflicted upon him and his siblings in their childhood. He had not admitted this, however, because he grew up in a strong religious atmosphere in which it was important to *honor* his father and mother.

Therefore, he said, instead of resenting his father, he hated authority. (It was significant that he used the word "resentment" toward his father and "hatred" toward authority.) He described difficult relationships he had with all of his teachers; how, as a teenager, he had conflicts with police; and how he could not develop a reasonable relationship with employers.

Michael summed up the problem by saying, "In my adult years, if I were to accept a position of real authority, it would mean

becoming the very thing that I hated." Since he had never acknowledged the conflict, he could not resolve it.

This was a shocking insight. He felt he had wasted 15 or more
years in not facing the problem. However, he shortly came to
grips with it and, before long, was able to establish a strong relationship with an entrepreneur who sold him his business on excellent
terms. From that point on, he had a very successful career, building and maintaining the business successfully for more than 20
years.

*Parents, with the best of intentions and inadvertently, explic-
itly, or more often unspokenly, put pressure on their children either to pursue certain specific careers, or to avoid others, or
both. Because of the parent/child bond, it is extremely difficult
for the child to oppose this persuasive force. Many children simply swallow their misgivings and accommodate themselves to
parental wishes. Others oppose the pressure but handle it poorly
in the emotion of the situation. Following is a case of a young
man who handled it in his own way:*

Acting Contrary to Parents' Hopes

In his early 20s, Joe had spent a number of years operating his
own one-person business, which had never been very successful.
His parents both were teachers in a local school system. He knew
very clearly that his parents' dream was that he, too, become a
teacher.

His sister had already given in to her parents' desire and was
unhappy as a teacher. In order to successfully combat the pressure from his parents, he dropped out of college after a year and a
half, fearing that if he did get a college degree, he might be unable
to resist. At the same time, he felt guilty about not acceding to
their wishes. This conflict kept him from succeeding in his business.

After examining his feelings on the subject, and after open
discussion with his parents, he decided to move to another state
many hundreds of miles away where he began to develop his career

strategy. He quickly involved himself in three new interests: Jewelry, music and shipping.

He called me before Christmas that same year to say that he was negotiating with the elderly owner of a retail jewelry chain who had in mind that this young man become an apprentice, preparing to assume the general management of the small chain of stores. It was my impression from the telephone conversation that he would accept the offer.

A year later, Joe wrote me a 12-page letter, written apparently after an exhausting but exhilarating day. He had not accepted the offer to become general manager of the jewelry store chain, but instead had moved into all three of his interests.

He was operating a promotional business, helping a number of musical groups to arrange their schedules. He had established a diamond importing business including several distributorships which he regularly supplied. And he and a shipper he had befriended were in the process of forming a ship salvage business together.

He closed his letter saying that he was working 18 hours a day, coming home at night tired but contented. Best of all, the resentment he had felt toward his parents was entirely gone. He now understood why they had felt as they did, and, since he now clearly knew what he wanted, they were proud of his success.

♦ TRAUMATIC EXPERIENCES AND DIFFICULT SITUATIONS

A career consultant becomes painfully aware of the cruelty which is inflicted on employees in the marketplace. These incidents leave wounds which eventually heal, but in some extreme cases, unfortunately, they apparently leave a permanent scar. It is fortunate that usually even the deepest of wounds can be healed if the victim will face the problem forthrightly.

Atrocities in the Marketplace

Many years ago, one of my clients told me a story which, to this day, remains the most vicious incident I have ever heard. It was a combination of failure to live up to promises, salaries not paid as they were due, mental torture, and even physical abuse.

When Jim entrusted his story to me, I was appalled at what I heard. Since it was a fairly recent episode, I asked him if he were still bitter about it. He told me resignedly that such was life and that he simply had to accept it and move onwards and upwards.

Even though he seemed to be handling it well, I suspected that he still brooded about the incident. Later, when he was having interviews, it became clear that he was not doing well. We scheduled a session on a Friday afternoon which would allow extended time to examine the problem.

It required only about a half an hour for him to reveal the depth of his bitterness and resentment. At the end of that time, his hands were shaking, his face was red, and he told me in a strained voice, "I'd like to take a baseball bat and cave in the heads of each of those men."

He went on haltingly to explain his real feelings about the episode. Not long after, having examined his feelings in depth, he was able to set them aside and go on from there. Until then, this subconscious wound "festered" to the point where he was unconsciously seeing a similar potential problem with everyone he met.

His interviews improved immediately. The positive reactions he began getting from others helped him to heal rapidly.

It is fortunate
that usually even the deepest of wounds
can be healed if the victim
will face the problem forthrightly.

Atrocities in the Market Place II

Episodes such as the one just discussed and the one that follows have convinced me that perhaps the most important meaning of the phrase "the truth shall set you free" has to do with our ability to honestly face the truth about ourselves no matter how painful it may be.

When he first came for help, Oliver was the manager of a city-wide branch of a major national firm. While he felt he had successfully increased the revenue for the office, he had detected some overtones in the past year that he was not in the best of graces with his own regional manager.

When he came to me for his third appointment, he was obviously upset. He told me that two days earlier, his regional manager had called him and told him to set up a breakfast meeting with his entire office staff, including all clerical workers. The regional manager himself and one other person would also attend.

At the meeting that very morning, after breakfast was over, the regional manager had stood and announced to the entire office staff that Oliver was being terminated effective immediately, and he introduced the new manager to the group. After the breakfast Oliver simply went back to his office and cleaned out his desk.

Oliver concluded later that he was abruptly terminated because his retirement program would soon be vested after 30 years of service to the company. The retirement plan would have given him in the neighborhood of $75,000 per year. Using a legal loophole available at the time, the company simply fired him, reimbursed his initial investment of about $10,000, and saved a considerable sum of money.

Oliver brooded for some time over what the company had done, but then began to rally. He started an entirely new career for himself and went on to become a successful, self-employed financial advisor.

One Client's Love-Hate Relationship with
   The Business World

The war in Vietnam had an adverse effect on thousands of lives. I have helped many people think through the aftermath of combat experiences in their lives.

However, some of the most negative effects of that conflict have been visited upon those who did not participate in the fighting, but remained home to go to school. Guilt developed in the minds of some of those who were college students at the time when many of their own age group were fighting and dying in Vietnam.

Peter was a very intelligent, highly trained individual. His work was always impeccably done. But he seemed unable to stay with a company much more than a year at a time. In some cases, he had been asked to leave after only a few months.

His method of dealing with people was abrasive. He was aloof, terse in his speaking style, and appeared to be putting most people down. He was painfully aware of the problem and wanted to do something about it. Fortunately for him, the last organization which terminated him as an employee paid the fees for his outplacement program.

He began to realize, after painful reflection, that he was in a love-hate relationship with the business world. As he explained, it was common doctrine on college campuses during the 1960s that the Vietnam conflict was unjustifiable, that the United States was clearly in the wrong, and that business and industry in providing support to that conflict were also in the wrong.

In Peter's adult years, this unconscious resentment was directed at every corporation, every business, every manager for whom he worked. This insight enabled him to re-think his attitude. He slowly but surely re-established good communications at work.

His style became less abrasive and his co-workers became more comfortable with him. His next position lasted for several years.

A very high percentage of the people I have worked with have had concerns about the ethics and professionalism of one or more of their companies. In some cases, they have been concerned about legality. For most of us, this creates a tough choice between the need to support ourselves and our families, and the need to distance ourselves from questionable ethical practices. The following case describes how one courageous person handled the problem:

Insurance Manager Works Through Ethical Concerns

Frank had a severe moral and ethical concern. As manager of a major territory within his national firm, he was responsible for the recruitment of successful businessmen for the sales force.

The company plan required him and his counterparts around the country to approach people with annual salaries of $30,000 to $40,000 and entice them to join his company with the thought that they could make twice as much or more in insurance sales. He said that while it was true that a small percentage of the people who made the shift were able to make that kind of money, the great majority of them made less than they had before.

As a result, his conscience bothered him. The turnover was somewhere in the neighborhood of 90 percent: For every ten new salesmen he took aboard in this fashion, a year later only one remained. The nine who left had worsened their personal positions considerably.

The experience had soured him so much that his intention was to leave the field entirely. Since he was a devout sports fan, he was determined somehow to build his career in that direction. He investigated the sports world, from promotion of sports to the production and distribution of athletic equipment and supplies.

His new search had gone on for about a month when he told me that his wife had rather timidly told him that she could understand his interest in sports because he had always been a fan, but she really couldn't see him peddling golf clubs. He knew immediately that she was right, and he re-thought his career decision once more.

In the final analysis, he realized that he should not allow the one experience to sour him on an entire industry. He decided he would find or negotiate a situation in the insurance industry where he could operate according to his own ethical and professional principles.

He found a company in which he could offer a direct salary base to people who were already successful. He found that salespeople starting with this foundation were more successful by far than the ones he had brought in before on a draw and straight commission. Those who were recruited were fully aware of the pitfalls, and at the same time had sufficient income to maintain their standard of living while developing a new ability. This method settled Frank's conscience

In the course of the next several years, he established several businesses of his own. A few years ago, in a chance meeting, he told me that he would never again allow himself to become as dependent on another entity or company as he was in the first situation described above.

♦ OUTPLACEMENT CASE STUDIES

Every company that terminates an employee after years of service owes it to that employee to help sever the bond which has developed over the years, and to deal with the emotions of that traumatic period. It is important that the principals (CEO, vice presidents) devote personal attention to this concern and not leave it to the human resource department.

A policy should be developed which provides an effective, efficient "bridge" for terminated employees to the next career position. It should be a "no fault" policy which requires every manager and employee of the company to treat employees who must be fired respectfully, and to consciously help such a person retain a solid, positive self-image in spite of the trauma of the separation.

About 40 percent of the clients I have worked with on an outplacement basis have stayed in the field of experience. Sixty percent have made some rather remarkable changes. When individuals come on their own for individual career counseling and guidance, about 80 percent have radically changed the direction of their careers.

Company President Fires Personnel Manager Is Himself Fired the Same Day

In a memorable outplacement case, Kevin, the president of a relatively large company in the medical field, asked me to help him terminate the personnel manager, a 12-year employee. Since Kevin intended to handle the termination interview himself, we combined the discussion of how to design the termination procedures with the coaching session to help him prepare for the termination interview.

On the day the firing was scheduled, I arrived at Kevin's office and, as planned, waited in an adjacent conference room where I was to meet with the employee immediately after the firing.

Fifteen minutes after the time scheduled, Kevin walked into the conference room, alone, with a distracted air about him. He said that he was uncertain whether or how to proceed. He himself, just moments before in an encounter in the hallway, had been fired by a member of the board. His termination was effective that same day at 5:00 p.m., and he would not be required to terminate the personnel manager.

After thinking out loud about it for a few minutes, Kevin decided to terminate the personnel manager himself because, he felt, the board might not provide career support services to this person.

He proceeded with the termination interview, and brought the personnel manager in to see me. He waited for me to complete that session so that he could talk to me again. Later he prevailed on the board of directors to provide the same kind of support for himself and contracted with me to provide it.

I arrived at the corporate offices at 1:00 p.m. that day and left for home about 6:15. It was a tiring afternoon, but a particularly satisfying one, in that I could help two people wrestle with a major traumatic incident and begin to take the next step in their careers.

**Every company should develop a policy
which provides an effective "bridge"
for terminated employees
to their next career position.**

The fired personnel manager decided to leave the medical world, moved toward broadcasting, and quickly found a top management position, at a higher salary, with a major television broadcasting company.

The fired president had a more difficult experience, but later opted for overseas work and at last report, was being considered for a health-related government post in a Mediterranean country.

It has been estimated that the true cost of an experienced employee's leaving a company ranges between $50,000 to $150,000. The accumulated knowledge lost to the company, the reduced efficiency while a replacement is being trained, the cost of training the replacement, the loss of employee morale among the remaining employees, the cost in public relations — all add up to a substantial figure.

In the following case, in which a fired employee was rehired, the cost of the career-guidance support for the terminated employee amounted to a pittance in light of the value of retaining a long-term employee, in repairing communication problems in a division of the company, in the increased enthusiasm and efficiency which was clearly exhibited by the employee.

Laid Off Employee Returns to Company In New Position

In a classic outplacement case, an 18-year employee, Mike, was let go by a large national manufacturing company because of inadequate performance. He was angry because he felt the real reason, under the surface, was a poor relationship with his immediate boss. In rethinking his situation, however, he began to realize that he had contributed as much, if not more, to the negative atmosphere as did his boss.

He began to realize that he had been disenchanted for some time with the type of work he did in the company, and he knew there were many managers in the organization whom he admired and respected.

As his resentment faded, he began to know that he was proud to be associated with the industry. He knew he had been proud to be associated with the company because it stands out nationally for the quality of its products, professionalism and integrity.

On his own initiative, he began to make contact with many of the top managers in the company and ultimately negotiated a different position for himself, in a different division, in another part of the country — and at a substantially higher salary than his previous one.

Quite a number of companies have told employees as they were terminated that they were free to retain my services at company expense if they so desired. Generally, there was no prior planning by the company as to how to handle each employee's case, and as I recall, the actual firings each took place on a Friday afternoon. Unfortunately, less than half of the people who were given the option of professional support actually took advantage of it.

One Manager's Unfortunate Case

In this example, the company called me on a Friday morning to say that they were going to terminate one of their managers that afternoon, and asked if I could come.

My schedule did not permit it, so I pleaded with them, for the sake of the employee, to wait until Monday or Tuesday. They said they would proceed with the firing that afternoon and tell the employee to see me the following Monday.

When I told them how often people in those circumstances fail to take advantage of such a service but elect to take some time off, they told me that with this particular employee there would be no problem. He would certainly come to see me immediately. The following Monday, I discovered that he had decided to go on a two-week fishing trip.

A month later, I called the company to inquire. After some delay, the company representative called me back to assure me that the fired employee would be in soon; he was simply involved in some home projects.

Still another month later, he had not made contact with me. The company representative, now embarrassed, finally visited the former employee at his home. More than three months after the termination had taken place, this former employee began working with me.

He was difficult to work with. He had spent several months trying to resolve his career problem without help. He had not healed from the rather severe ego-battering which occurred at the time he was fired.

In the final analysis, he resolved the problem and found a better career position. But the cost was high in terms of embarrassment to the company, to the employee's self-image, and to his wife and family. The company representative found it necessary to leave behind a less-than-accurate record of the incident in order to protect himself.

Outplacement Assistance Makes the Difference

In another case, a company terminated an executive and his immediate subordinate. The company simply suggested to these people that they were quite welcome to use my services at the company's expense.

The subordinate did work with me and was able to make a smooth transition to another position. But his former boss could not bring himself to come in. A friend tried several times to persuade him, but to no avail. I received occasional reports from my client on the situation.

After about a year, he told me that his former boss had lost his beach house and property, and then, after going through a second mortgage on his house in town, lost that, too.

After about a year-and-a-half, this man still had no means of income. His marriage had ended in divorce and he was nearly destitute. I am convinced that if that man had sought immediate help — or if the company had insisted — he would have saved his marriage, his property and his self-esteem.

A Manager Saved From Firing,
Much Later Terminated

Jack is a very large man who stands about 6'8" and probably weighs 300 pounds without an ounce of fat. He is a very nice man of the tough-but-oh-so-gentle variety.

One of the executives of his company, in his concern for Jack, contacted me to say that Jack was one of the finest managers in the company, but he was politically naive. Another executive in the company was orchestrating events to make Jack look bad. I was commissioned to help him with his political naivete and strengthen his position in the company.

In a very short time Jack understood the problem. He corrected the situation, and he spent three more productive years with the company. Several years later however, when the company cut back severely, Jack was one of those chosen to be cut.

The president hired me to help Jack with his transition. Once he recovered from the initial shock, he became a very powerful person, not only physically but also mentally and emotionally. He had spent nearly 20 years with the one company, and without realizing it, was mentally trapped within it.

When he reassessed his own abilities more realistically, he realized that he probably could have been president of the company he left. However, being a modest man, he had always cast himself in a subordinate role.

He took a better position with another company in another state. And at the same time, he is building his own new company.

Long-term unemployment can have a devastating impact on self-esteem, self-confidence, health and physical energy. It is re-markable how often people who are without work will let weeks turn into months and even years without seeking any kind of help to resolve the problem. In most other aspects of our lives, we more easily and readily seek help. The following case illustrates how devastating the unemployed situation can be, and how quickly the problem can be reversed.

Unemployed Controller Becomes Assistant General Manager Then Executive Vice President

Bart was deeply depressed when he first sought help with his career. Three years earlier he had been fired from a company in which he had been controller for more than ten years.

In three years of searching for a job, he had found nothing. His inability to find work was preying on him, causing him to worry all day long and to spend his nights tossing and turning. He had no energy and no motivation.

After his first year of looking for a position, he had decided to go into real estate. He and his wife obtained real estate licenses and went into business together. Then, compounding his problem, his wife was considerably more successful in real estate than he was.

After two years of what he perceived as failure in real estate, he finally sought help.

During our sessions, he identified a severe self-image problem which he had never before admitted. As it all surfaced, he wrote more than 20 pages describing the vulnerable feelings which had been with him all of his life and had held him back.

When he started his interview program, he did not take the initial, less demanding interview steps which I recommend. Without my knowing it, he made direct contact with the vice president and general manager of a branch of a large corporation located in the city. Bart had applied to that same company a year to a year-and-a-half earlier and had received no response.

His first meeting with the general manager went so well that for the first time in many years, he was able to swallow the lump in his throat and feel a surge of confidence. His second interview with the same man went even better. After each interview he told me with growing confidence that he was certain he would be offered a position.

**Long-term unemployment
can have a devastating impact
on self-esteem, self-confidence,
health and physical energy.**

After a seventh good interview with the same man, he still had no offer and was badly distressed. Since he was in danger of falling back into the same state of mind he was in when he first came for help, I advised him to press strongly for a decision from the general manager. He agreed and carefully planned his approach.

He told the general manager that since the second or third visit, he had felt he wanted to work in that company if there was a place for him. Did the general manager realize this? Yes. He also believed that the general manager intended to hire him. Was this true? Yes. The two proceeded to finalize their understanding. He was told to begin work the following Monday.

After starting to work, Bart realized that his new boss found it unusually difficult to fire people. He therefore had procrastinated in hiring Bart — because he needed to terminate an inefficient employee. Since there were far many more employees in the company than were actually needed, Bart began to recommend restructuring, including cutbacks, which resulted in a 10 percent improvement in the bottom line of the organization.

Bart was promoted within six months to the post of assistant to the general manager. About three years after he came aboard, when the company was merged with another company, both Bart and his boss were laid off.

Several weeks into his search for a new position, Bart excitedly called to tell me that he had just taken a position as executive vice president of a holding company which had five subsidiary companies. And he had doubled his previous salary.

I congratulated him and asked him how many interviews he had before being offered that position. He said it took 13 interviews. In the first eight to ten interviews, he was offered three separate positions, each of which he declined.

On the twelfth visit, the president offered him a position as executive vice president with responsibility to restructure the financial systems of the holding company and all its subsidiary companies. To finalize an offer of that kind, the president was required to seek approval from the chairman of the board, which occurred on the thirteenth interview.

It took a great deal of courage and tenacity for Bart to deal directly and honestly with the depths of his problem. But in approximately four years, he became a confident, competent top executive. He and people like him who face themselves and their weaknesses demonstrate that any of us can meet such challenges and improve our lives and careers.

**Three things are required
for a person to have a successful career:
Talent, self-honesty, and commitment.
Everyone has talent in some degree.
None of us is entirely honest with ourselves,
but any of us can improve that ability.
But the commitment to improve ourselves,
to make a change,
requires fierce determination and courage.**

EPILOGUE

---

*We must regain our ability
to control our own destinies,
our lives, and our careers.*

Change is the order of the day. Preparing ourselves for it, and courageously meeting its challenge, will carry us safely into the next century — and beyond.

The most profound change we must make is two-fold: The way we perceive ourselves, and the way we perceive each other.

In the past 100 years — encouraged by our institutions — we have been led into the trap of perceiving ourselves simply as the sum of our past activities. We need to recapture a vision of ourselves as individuals with fertile imaginations, with the ability to grow. We need the same vision of each other.

As we broaden our horizons, we will open ourselves up to a greater span of alternatives in the marketplace, a wider range of opportunities for personal and professional success.

Change is upon us. It is time for us to take control of our own destinies.

If you would like to order
additional copies of this book,
please call, toll-free:

1-800-343-1949

We're interested in your career development!
If you have any comments or questions about this
book, stories you'd like to share about your own
job-hunting experiences, or for more information on
Dr. Kevane's career advisory services,
please write or call:

R. A. Kevane & Associates
801 Second Avenue Suite 211
Seattle, Washington 98104

Tel: (206) 343-5828
Fax: (206) 343-7460